P9-DHJ-379

AN ESSAY ON THE ART OF INGENIOUSLY TORMENTING

JANE COLLIER was baptized in January 1715 at Steeple Langford in Wiltshire, one of four children of the philosopher and clergyman, the Reverend Arthur Collier. Her family moved to lodgings in Salisbury in 1716 when they encountered financial difficulties, and it was here that Collier grew up and was educated. Jane, along with her sister Margaret, learned Latin and Greek from her father, who died in 1732. Collier moved to London in the 1740s, where she met and became a trusted friend of some of the most prominent writers of her time, including Samuel Richardson and Henry and Sarah Fielding. Her first published work was *An Essay on the Art of Ingeniously Tormenting* (1753). She later collaborated with Sarah Fielding on her only other surviving work, *The Cry* (1754). Collier never married, and she died in London in 1755.

KATHARINE A. CRAIK completed her doctoral research at King's College Cambridge and is a Lecturer and Junior Research Fellow at Worcester College Oxford. She has published on Shakespeare, Spenser, Jonson, and their contemporaries and is writing a book entitled *Writing, Sensation, and the Origins of Pornography in Early Modern England*.

OXFORD WORLD'S CLASSICS

*For over 100 years Oxford World's Classics have brought
readers closer to the world's great literature. Now with over 700
titles—from the 4,000-year-old myths of Mesopotamia to the
twentieth century's greatest novels—the series makes available
lesser-known as well as celebrated writing.*

*The pocket-sized hardbacks of the early years contained
introductions by Virginia Woolf, T. S. Eliot, Graham Greene,
and other literary figures which enriched the experience of reading.
Today the series is recognized for its fine scholarship and
reliability in texts that span world literature, drama and poetry,
religion, philosophy and politics. Each edition includes perceptive
commentary and essential background information to meet the
changing needs of readers.*

OXFORD WORLD'S CLASSICS

JANE COLLIER

An Essay on the Art of Ingeniously Tormenting

Edited with an Introduction and Notes by
KATHARINE A. CRAIK

OXFORD
UNIVERSITY PRESS

OXFORD

UNIVERSITY PRESS

Great Clarendon Street, Oxford OX2 6DP

Oxford University Press is a department of the University of Oxford.
It furthers the University's objective of excellence in research, scholarship,
and education by publishing worldwide in

Oxford New York

Auckland Cape Town Dar es Salaam Hong Kong Karachi
Kuala Lumpur Madrid Melbourne Mexico City Nairobi
New Delhi Shanghai Taipei Toronto

With offices in

Argentina Austria Brazil Chile Czech Republic France Greece
Guatemala Hungary Italy Japan Poland Portugal Singapore
South Korea Switzerland Thailand Turkey Ukraine Vietnam

Oxford is a registered trade mark of Oxford University Press
in the UK and in certain other countries

Published in the United States
by Oxford University Press Inc., New York

© Katharine A. Craik 2006

British Library Cataloguing in Publication Data

Data available

Library of Congress Cataloging in Publication Data

Collier, Jane, 1715?–1755.
An essay on the art of ingeniously tormenting / Jane Collier ; edited with an introduction
and notes by Katharine A. Craik.
p. cm. — (Oxford world's classics)
Includes bibliographical references.
1. Women—Conduct of life—Humor—Early works to 1800. 2. Interpersonal relations—Humor—
Early works to 1800. 3. Conduct of life—Humor—Early works to 1800. I. Craik, Katharine A.
II. Title. III. Oxford world's classics (Oxford University Press)
PN6231.W6C65 2006 824'.6—dc22 2005030186

Typeset in Ehrhardt
by RefineCatch Limited, Bungay, Suffolk
Printed in Great Britain by
Clays Ltd, St. Ives plc.

ISBN 0–19–280552–5 978–0–19–280552–2

To my husband Steve,
patient recipient of many an ingenious torment

ACKNOWLEDGEMENTS

I would like to thank Markman Ellis for introducing me to Jane Collier and for reading the introduction to this edition, Martin Butler for tracking down Collier's reference to Ben Jonson, and Judith Luna at OUP for her many excellent suggestions and corrections. I am particularly grateful to Elizabeth and Alexander Craik who helped with the introduction and much more besides.

CONTENTS

INTRODUCTION

JANE COLLIER's *An Essay on the Art of Ingeniously Tormenting* is a courageous social satire published at a time when satires were usually written by and for men. It is also an advice book, a handbook of anti-etiquette, and an energetic comedy of manners. Although addressed in part to husbands and fathers, *The Art* was written first and foremost for an audience of women in their capacity as wives, mothers, friends, and the mistresses of servants. Collier engages with some of the most pressing debates of her time including the controversy surrounding women's education, questions of civility and good manners, and emerging notions of bourgeois domesticity. Responding wittily and often savagely to available paradigms of feminine virtue, Collier jettisons ladylike meekness in favour of assertiveness, docility in favour of bloody-mindedness, and rational behaviour in favour of studied petulance. Describing methods for 'teasing and mortifying' (p. 17) others in a variety of different social situations by laying traps for their desires and affections, Collier tutors her readers in how to make themselves an insufferable nuisance to everyone around them. *The Art* provides a fascinating glimpse into the imaginative life of an intelligent eighteenth-century woman. It also suggests, in colourful terms, the difficulties women experienced in exerting their influence in private and public life—and the ways they got round them. Collier's frank, outspoken voice gave her the freedom not only to dispense with social constraints, particularly those affecting women, but also to put a match to such constraints and gleefully watch them burn.

The authors of conduct books for ladies had been arguing for decades that behaving in an ungovernable fashion made women a torment to themselves as well as to others. In *The Ladies Calling*, an influential book of advice first published in 1673, Richard Allestree had suggested that 'a woman's tongue should indeed be like the imaginary Music of the spheres, sweet and charming, but

not to be heard at distance'.[1] Women should strive quietly for
exemplary virtue, avoiding bickering and scoffing, and banishing
all indecency, rudeness, or superciliousness from their conversation together with any impudent tendency to impose their
opinions on others. Collier was familiar with the tradition of
advice-giving in which Allestree's book played an important part,
but her own approach in *The Art* is fresh and original. She seizes
upon precisely those shortcomings in women's characters which
Allestree soberly warned against, describing with relish their
bothersome repercussions for families, friendships, and polite
society at large. Instead of sketching exemplary womanhood in
all its illustrious (and insipid) goodness, Collier writes a witty
exposé of everything deplorable in human nature. Although she
anatomizes the 'pleasant art' of emotional abuse partly in order to
pique readers into acknowledging their own faults, Collier is
never censorious or didactic. Rather she persuades us that 'plaguing, teasing, or tormenting' (p. 6) are useful and ingenious arts
even as she reproves their effects. Her work seems animated less
by the impulse to expose women's frailties than to lay bare the
humourless and patronizing double standards which under-
pinned many contemporary assumptions about femininity.

Women were entering the marketplace of print in
unprecedented numbers in the mid-eighteenth century with
literary and non-literary works including prose fiction, poetry,
plays, journalistic essays, and instructional treatises. Britain's
leisure industry was developing, education and literacy were
improving, and London's book trade was flourishing under
revised copyright laws and the decline of aristocratic patronage.[2]
Although women were writing more books than ever before, they
had to work hard to justify their appearance in print. Many drew
attention to their virtuous motives such as a humble desire to
teach others, or appealed in prefaces to their readers' charity by
describing their financial distress and explaining that they were

---

[1] Richard Allestree, *The Ladies Calling* (1673), 7.

[2] On changes in the eighteenth-century English economy, and how these affected
women's writing, see Cheryl Turner, *Living by the Pen: Women Writers in the Eighteenth
Century* (London: Routledge, 1992), 13–14.

obliged to publish in order to support fatherless children, sick husbands, or dying parents.[3] Such conventions recall the prejudices female writers had encountered in the past; and although many of these constraints had now been lifted women were still expected to write reluctantly and to showcase delicacy, sensitivity, and moral spotlessness. Bearing this in mind, Collier's achievement is particularly remarkable. She must have encountered intense pressure to conform, and her personal circumstances hardly put her in a secure risk-taking position. But she seems determined to expose in *The Art* the absurdity of readers' continued attachment to certain aspects of 'sentimental' femininity even as women were negotiating confident, professional identities in print. She fully appreciated the significance of writing as an act of self-assertion—especially the risks women took in exposing themselves to criticism by writing satire.

Jane Collier

Jane Collier was baptized on 16 January 1715 at Langford Magna (now Steeple Langford) in Wiltshire, the daughter of the philosopher and clergyman, the Reverend Arthur Collier (1680–1732), and Margaret Johnson who died in 1749. She had two brothers, Arthur and Charles, and one sister, Margaret. While Jane was still a baby, the Colliers suffered a serious downturn in fortunes, probably caused in part by her mother's profligacy. As a result her father was forced to let the family's house at Langford and to sell their long-standing right to the parish.[4] In 1716 the family moved into more modest quarters in Salisbury, and it was here that Jane grew up and was educated. The family's circumstances improved little in the years which followed: Arthur multiplied the debt he inherited from his father and, in 1745,

[3] Janet Todd discusses 'the modest muse' in chapter 7 of *The Sign of Angellica: Women, Writing, and Fiction, 1660–1800* (London: Virago, 1989), esp. p. 126.

[4] On Collier's early life and family circumstances, see Betty Rizzo, *Companions Without Vows: Relationships among Eighteenth-Century British Women* (Athens, Ga. and London: University of Georgia Press, 1994), 337 n. 8; and Tom Keymer, 'Jane Collier, Reader of Richardson, and the Fire Scene in *Clarissa*', in Albert J. Rivero (ed.), *New Essays on Samuel Richardson* (Basingstoke: Macmillan, 1996), 141–61, at 144–5.

found himself embroiled in legal proceedings with his creditors. Jane and her siblings were faced with the responsibility of earning their own livings: Arthur became a lawyer at the ecclesiastical court of Doctors' Commons, Charles joined the army, and Margaret became a governess to the novelist Henry Fielding's daughter Harriet—an appointment which ended in disaster.[5] Jane herself does not seem to have secured any such employment and faced the socially difficult condition of spinsterhood at a time when the security of women depended upon their ability to marry well. When her brother Charles died on active service in Nova Scotia he left his estate to his two sisters, but the sum was clearly insufficient to relieve them from financial uncertainty.[6] Jane spent much of her life living with friends and relatives, relying on their charity much like the 'humble companions' she describes in *The Art* (p. 21). Perhaps she, like her friend Sarah Fielding, remained unmarried because she was unable to offer a sufficient dowry. Or perhaps she chose not to marry, hoping to carve out an independent living by her pen and wit.[7]

Fortunately Jane had a wide and affectionate circle of friends. She met Samuel Richardson in the late 1740s while he was writing *Clarissa*, and later became one of his trusted friends and advisers. She may have been living as a member of his household around the time she was writing *The Art*, and Richardson assisted her by printing it for the publisher Andrew Millar. Richardson's fondness for Jane is suggested in a letter he wrote to Sarah Fielding after her death: 'Don't you miss our dear Miss Jenny Collier more and more?—I do.'[8] Henry Fielding too admired Jane's

[5] Margaret travelled with Fielding and his family to Portugal in 1754. Shortly before his death Fielding accused her of conspiring with his second wife, Mary Daniel, to usurp his authority by ruining his reputation among the English community at Lisbon. Judith Hawley discusses Fielding's dramatic falling-out with Margaret in her edition of *The Art of Ingeniously Tormenting* (Bristol: Thoemmes Press, 1994), pp. ix–x. See also Martin C. Battestin with Ruthe R. Battestin, *Henry Fielding, A Life* (London: Routledge, 1989; repr. 1993), 393 and 599–600.

[6] Keymer, 'Jane Collier, Reader of Richardson', 145.

[7] The condition of spinsterhood is discussed in Bridget Hill's *Women Alone: Spinsters in England, 1660–1850* (New Haven and London: Yale University Press, 2001).

[8] Richardson included Collier's initials on the list of esteemed women he drew up in 1750. See T. C. Duncan Eaves and Ben D. Kimpel, *Samuel Richardson: A Biography*

intellect and virtues; she became a familiar among his circle of literary associates and lived during the early 1750s with his sister Sarah. The two women worked together closely on Collier's only other surviving literary work, an experimental dramatic fable entitled *The Cry* (1754). A densely literary and philosophically complex work, *The Cry* describes the struggle of its heroines, Portia and Cylinda, against the 'spiteful and malicious tongues' of an unprincipled society. Collier and Fielding shared an original, sparky intelligence and a conviction that fiction could improve readers' moral integrity. If Collier had not died in her early forties, her contribution to eighteenth-century literature would no doubt have been even more significant: her common-place book records that she planned a sequel, 'A book called *The Laugh* on the same plan as *The Cry*'.[9]

The Art was first published in 1753 and Collier's preface to the second edition suggests that it sold well. Like many other eighteenth-century books, especially satires, it was published anonymously. Its popularity and continuing appeal are suggested by the number of times it was reprinted: two editions appeared in 1753, an expanded second edition in 1757, and another seven editions before 1811. Collier describes her work as deliberately provisional, for *The Art* is merely a set of observations 'collected together, in one small pocket volume' (p. 6). Nor does she stake any claim to newness, presuming instead that her readers are already proficient in the techniques she describes. *The Art* is a collection of fail-safe tactics—or, to put it another way, a record of the methods of tormenting which readers have already perfected. Collier traces three distinct opportunities for teasing and

(Oxford: Clarendon Press, 1971), 343; and Hawley (ed.), *The Art of Ingeniously Tormenting*, p. viii. Richardson's letter is found in *The Correspondence of Samuel Richardson*, ed. Anna Laetitia Barbauld, 6 vols. (London: Richard Phillips, 1804), ii. 104.

[9] Carolyn Woodward questioned whether the attribution to Collier and Fielding was wholly correct in 'Who Wrote *The Cry*?: A Fable for Our Times', *Eighteenth-Century Fiction*, 9/1 (1996), 91–7. But Collier's central involvement now seems certain, thanks to the recent discovery of her commonplace book. The manuscript is in the possession of Dr Michael Londry of the Department of English, University of Alberta, Canada; he discusses his discovery in 'Our Dear Miss Jenny Collier', *TLS* (5 March 2004), 13–14. The quotation from *The Cry* appears in vol. i, p. 13.

plaguing other people. The first derives from the 'exterior power' or authority secured by law or convention such as that enjoyed by masters over their servants, parents over their children, and husbands over their wives. The second, an 'interior power', arises from the affections of others such as husbands' fondness for their wives or the good regard of friends for one another. The third more general opportunity for tormenting arises from the expectation of goodwill which customarily binds all acquaintances to one another. Together these three opportunities cover the whole sphere of human relations and, in every case, Collier advises her students to study others' vulnerabilities, needling and nettling them so cleverly that this art of insolence remains undetectable. *The Art* is full of absorbing reflections on eighteenth-century daily life, the treatment of servants and dependants, and the bringing up of children. To today's readers Collier's advice is still as wickedly funny and subtly subversive as it ever was.

Sentiment and Introspection

Collier was responding in *The Art* to a long tradition of writings about introspection. Conduct books advising readers how to cultivate their manners, refine their speech, and deal judiciously with others in domestic and professional situations had grown popular in the late sixteenth and early seventeenth centuries. Most were intended for aristocratic gentlemen readers, but those addressed to women emphasized the particular importance of moral integrity. In the first decades of the eighteenth century, large numbers of books were dedicated to remaking women's characters and to establishing new guidelines for feminine propriety.[10] Many were written by women for women, such as Elizabeth Singer Rowe's prescriptive *Friendship in Death* (1728) and *Devout Exercises of the Heart* (1738) and, later, Elizabeth Griffith's *Essays Addressed to Young Married Women* (1782). From an

---

[10] On eighteenth-century advice books for women, see Turner, *Living by the Pen*, 20. For a discussion of women's modesty in fiction and culture, see Ruth Bernard Yeazell, *Fictions of Modesty: Women and Courtship in the English Novel* (Chicago and London: University of Chicago Press, 1991).

initial emphasis upon moral reflection, this body of work later stressed women's 'sensibility' or keen sensitivity towards anything affecting in life or art, an ideal which was to remain central to English literature and culture until the 1790s. Writers described women's notional susceptibility to emotions and feelings, especially pity and sympathy, dwelling upon the tenderness of their bodies and their correspondingly sensitive minds and souls. In *Sermons to Young Women* (1766), James Fordyce praised women's 'complacence, yieldingness, and sweetness', especially the 'requisite and natural' qualities of a gentle voice and demeanour, and a delicate-looking frame. Women's innate compassion and spontaneous intuition was literally visible in their tendency towards blushing and 'melting of the eyes' in tears, for the female sex 'being of softer mold, is more pliant and yielding to the impressions of pitty, and by the strength of fancy redoubles the horror of any sad object'.[11] Modesty and obedience were inseparable from piety and chastity, and women were praised (or criticized) according to their ability to combine sentimental qualities with the highest standards of moral refinement.

Fiction published at this time reflects the taste for books designed to improve readers' morals. Novels deliberated the virtues of prudence, modesty, and reserve, and the fascination with exemplary human nature, broadly conceived, is evident in titles such as Sarah Fielding's *The Adventures of David Simple* (1744)—the book which provided Collier with her title for *The Art*—and Eliza Haywood's *The History of Miss Betsy Thoughtless* (1751).[12] Richardson's *Clarissa* (1747–8) and *Pamela* (1749) and Jean-Jacques Rousseau's *Émile* (1762), popular in English translation, all supplied stories laced with moral didacticism about the lives of women. These works continued to privilege sentiment

[11] James Fordyce, *Sermons to Young Women*, 2 vols. (1766), vol. ii, sermon 12 'On Female Meekness', 262 and 265; Allestree, *The Ladies Calling*, 49.

[12] On the ' "moral" tone in fiction,' see Turner, *Living by the Pen*, 53. Collier's title is drawn from *David Simple*, bk. 2, ch. 7: here Cynthia explains to David that the attitude of unscrupulous patrons towards their dependants is based on a studied 'Art of tormenting'. See *The Adventures of David Simple*, ed. Linda Bree (London: Penguin, 2002), 103. Audrey Bilger discusses Collier's title in her edition of *The Art of Ingeniously Tormenting* (Peterborough, Ont.: Broadview Press, 2003), 16.

but also redressed what Janet Todd has called the 'the apolitical self-indulgence associated with the Cult of Sensibility' by exploring the crises which arise when moral and religious principles clash with the desire for self-fulfilment.[13] Sentimental femininity no longer looked merely charming, but could now be seen to exact a price on individuals and society at large. Like many of her contemporaries who wrote fiction, Collier regarded sentimental femininity as psychologically and culturally significant. Unlike most of them, however, she was interested in sentimental femininity primarily as a rich resource for satire. She clearly had no truck with the fantasy created by writers such as Frances Brooke and the Minifie sisters, Margaret and Susanna: that timid, passive women who suffer distress patiently are always rewarded in the end. When Collier suggests briskly that readers would do well to act 'in direct opposition to all that a Swift, an Addison, a Richardson, a Fielding, or any other good ethical writer intended to teach' (p. 98) she departs from the assumptions of her contemporaries, and anticipates the fierce wit and social realism of later fiction dealing with the predicaments of women, especially the novels of Fanny Burney and Jane Austen. It seems likely that Austen had *The Art* in mind when she created the arch tormentor Mary Musgrove in *Persuasion*.[14]

The question of whether women's sentiments were 'naturally' superior to men's was much debated at the time Collier was writing *The Art*. Her contemporaries insisted that women were bound by a stricter moral code because of their innate sweetness of disposition.[15] It was not enough for them temporarily to assume a good nature or to pretend falsely to have acquired one, for only effortlessly and artlessly achieved goodness was worth cherishing. Allestree spoke for many when he argued that 'as far as Affability partakes of Humility it must of Sincerity also, that being a vertu whose very elements are plainness and simplicity: for as it has no designs which want a cover, so it needs none of those subtilties and simulations, those pretences and artifices

---

[13] Todd, *The Sign of Angellica*, 161.

[14] Keymer, 'Jane Collier, Reader of Richardson', 147.

[15] On this double standard, see Todd, *The Sign of Angellica*, 109.

requisite to those that do.[16] In *The Female Spectator* (1744–6), the first periodical written by and for women, Eliza Haywood agreed that 'an affability of manners and behaviour, or what is vulgarly called *good nature* . . . must be permanent, sincere, not assumed or affected, but flowing from a real benevolence of mind, which takes delight in contributing all it can to the welfare of others'. It is on the contrary 'a fiend-like disposition to be pleased with giving pain'. Sour humour turns women into viragos or men-women, giving them wrinkles, causing their cheeks to sink, their eyes to become inflamed, and their complexions to fade. Such a disposition may be bestowed at birth, or may be learned subsequently: 'There are two sources from whence what is called *ill nature* proceeds; the one, is from the seeds of tyranny in the soul; the other, only from habit or accidents.'[17] Whereas the first is largely unstoppable, the second may be softened through the exercise of reason and reflection. Collier was particularly interested in these questions of sincerity and authenticity. To what extent is feminine perfection (or indeed a fiend-like disposition) inherited, and to what extent can it be learned or perfected? Is it possible to determine the difference between an affected goodness (or badness) and one which is permanent and sincere? Whereas Haywood hoped that women would nurture the 'modest timidity' they had been born with, Collier experimented further with the idea that maliciousness, like modesty, is 'implanted in our natures' (p. 6).[18] She replaces the familiar set of feminine charms with an equally familiar set of feminine faults, cleverly retaining the hyperbole of sentimental femininity whilst unpicking its basic assumptions. The task at hand in *The Art* is not how to be kind, but rather how craftily to cultivate a reputation for kindliness which serves the tormentor's own ends. By rethinking the notion of innateness, Collier exposes the hypocrisy at the heart of the view that feminine virtue comes somehow more naturally to women than to men—especially when that

[16] Allestree, *The Ladies Calling*, 69.

[17] Patricia Meyer Spacks (ed.), *Selections from The Female Spectator* (Oxford: Oxford University Press, 1999), 72, 75, 78, and 76.

[18] Ibid. 297.

view is held by men who set about the task of teaching women natural modesty.

Conduct books for men had evolved into satires by the mid-eighteenth century. Collier knew Jonathan Swift's *Directions to Servants* (1745), an essay which sends up conventional advice books by purporting to teach servants how to perpetrate 'villainies and frauds' against their masters and mistresses. But conduct books for women remained popular, often analysing women's follies (vanity, greed, impiousness, irrationality) with a view to mending them.[19] Collier follows a radically different method. Devoting her entire book to cataloguing the delights of tormenting others, Collier implies that traditional conduct books are woefully inadequate to mend a natural bent towards mischief-making and should therefore be read only as a guide to how not to behave. The sentimental woman was expected to be ceaselessly vigilant over the effects of her company on others, taking every opportunity to gladden, solace, and comfort those around her. Collier turns this watchfulness around: the proficient tormentor is aware of the impressions she makes, but uses this awareness to determine her most effective strategy. She may begin her campaign by flattering and cajoling, but then display an abrupt 'change of temper' (p. 64). Sincere-seeming kindness is therefore only a method of ensnaring dupes upon whom she plans to 'exercise the utmost brutality, under the name of plain-dealing' (p. 66). The more accurate her assessments of their characters and dispositions, the more keenly the effects of her strokes will be felt—and the greater her pleasure in mortifying her prey.

The authors of conduct books often emphasized the value of female friendship. James Fordyce described the qualities women should look for and nurture in one another, namely openheartedness, discretion, steadiness, cheerfulness, and wisdom

[19] *Directions to Servants and Miscellaneous Pieces 1733–1742*, vol. xiii of *The Prose Works of Jonathan Swift*, ed. Herbert Davis (Oxford: Basil Blackwell, 1939). The quotation is from 'The Publisher's Preface' by George Faulkner, p. 5. The evolution of conduct literature is traced in Nancy Armstrong and Leonard Tennenhouse (eds.), *The Ideology of Conduct: Essays on Literature and the History of Sexuality* (New York and London: Methuen, 1987); see esp. Armstrong's chapter, 'The Rise of the Domestic Woman', 96–141.

without censoriousness.[20] Rather than privileging alliances between women, like Fordyce, or striving benevolently to find reasons to like others, as Haywood recommended, Collier instead suggests ways women might identify, nourish, and then capitalize on their reasons for disliking each other—especially if these reasons are groundless.[21] She teaches her apprentice tormentors to be mindful that *'those injuries go nearest to us, that we neither deserve nor expect'* (p. 66). A woman is easily mortified about her clothes since the tormentor may simply claim to have seen some unfashionable person wearing the very same gown or cap. She is readily embarrassed when her careful efforts to attract suitors are exposed, and the proficient tormentor may even find ways to steal her intended lover or, if that fails, of cooling his affections towards her. If she finds herself in the company of someone deli-cate or infirm, she may recommend all sorts of vigorous activities such as walking in the heat, staying out in a damp evening, and hurrying from place to place. If the indisposed party objects, 'you may accuse her of affectation, and a design of spoiling company' (p. 87). A woman of feeling therefore makes a richly rewarding tormentee, whereas picking a target with no tender affections means that 'all your sport is lost; and you might as well shoot your venom at a marble statue in your garden' (p. 23). Here the blush is not a sign of authentic feminine feeling but a valuable currency to exact from other women. The vulnerable female body and her correspondingly passive disposition are no longer respected on their own terms but are instead treasured as sources of malicious merry-making. But Collier's exposure of the hypocrisies behind society's attachment to sentimentality is never itself malicious. For in *The Art* she imagines a new mode of femininity which is self-aware, self-confident, and (above all) morally robust—even as she vividly sketches its opposite. Her tough reasoning assumes that women are capable of moral intelligence and are there-fore responsible for altering society's opinion of them, and allows

[20] Fordyce, *Sermons to Young Women*, vol. i, sermon 5 'On Female Virtue, Friendship, and Conversation', esp. p. 171.

[21] See Haywood's essay against prejudice in Spacks (ed.), *Selections from The Female Spectator*, 259–83.

her to retain the meaningful aspects of feminine sentiment—
goodwill, sympathy, tolerance—while dispensing with those she
considered narrow-minded and outmoded.

Domesticity

The Art reflects the fact that the lives of most middle-class
Englishwomen centred around the home. Women were often
entrusted with the efficient running of the household and under-
took some domestic work. Although (or perhaps because) their
social and professional freedoms were limited, the moral status of
women within the home rose dramatically in the early to mid-
eighteenth century.[22] As early as 1673, Allestree was arguing the
importance of domestic life to the welfare of society at large: 'the
Estate of Republicks entirely hangs on private families, the little
Monarchies both composing and giving Law unto the great.'
George Lyttleton's later poem, *Advice to a Lady* (1733), is a paean
to 'domestic worth' based on the assumption that 'A woman's
noblest station is retreat'.[23] Richardson's *Pamela* and many
other novels reflected and refracted these beliefs, favouring the
household as a scene of drama and concentrating on essentially
private relationships such as courtship, marriage, and parenthood. Collier's epigraph from Horace's *Ars Poetica*, 'Celebrare
domestica facta' (Celebrate domestic affairs), printed on the fron-
tispiece of the 1753 edition and repeated in 1757, confirms that
domesticity is a central concern of *The Art*. But the quotation
from Horace is accompanied by another from *The Child's Guide*:
'The Cat doth play, | And after slay.' Together these two frag-
ments raise and then find fault with the notion of noble, exalted
domesticity. Part of the satire of *The Art* is indeed directed
against those who regarded home-making as inevitably en-
nobling, for Collier bluntly confronts the problem of making
meaningful a life spent at home.

---

[22] Turner, *Living by the Pen*, 43.

[23] Allestree, *The Ladies Calling*, sig. b2ᵛ (unpaginated); George Lyttleton, *Advice to a Lady*, 6.

Some women extended the confines of their worlds by reading or seeking out stimulating company, but Collier's 'solution' is radically different. In *The Art*, the very qualities which many believed suited women to domestic rather than public life (especially modesty and self-abnegation), as well as their supposed flaws, are turned against those who might otherwise have profited from their confinement. Collier pokes fun at the idea that marriage was a union based on mutual respect which nevertheless depended upon women's wills being duly submissive to those of their 'lawfull Superiors'.[24] The chapter addressed to husbands is very brief for, Collier reasons, 'the sport of Tormenting is not the husband's chief game' (p. 43). A longer chapter for wives is included in the second part of *The Art*, devoted to the power conferred upon tormentors by the affections of others. Here women are advised to exploit the opportunities offered freely by husbands who 'either through affection, or indolence, have given up their legal rights; and have, by custom, placed all the power in the wife' (p. 43). If her husband is fond of music, his wife may persuade the children to create a noisy distraction. If he wants to talk quietly to her, she may immediately find something more pressing to attend to. If she finds herself in the company of his friends, she may plague her husband by being insufferably rude to them. Even gestures of affection present opportunities for 'deep malignant pleasure' (p. 51): a wife may bamboozle her husband into submission by kissing him, hanging around his neck, and bestowing more tormenting endearments upon him than a swarm of hornets, all the time working up his fondness for her—for one of the techniques most worth perfecting is that of 'forcing the offended person to ask pardon of the first aggressor'. *The Art* even contains some rather sinister advice about how to give the false impression of starving oneself, a technique guaranteed to cause any husband 'no small uneasiness' (p. 58). In short, the tormentor assiduously studies her husband's temper 'in order never to do any one thing that will please him' (p. 55).

Eighteenth-century satires are full of descriptions of such

---

[24] The quotation is from Allestree's *The Ladies Calling*, 39.

household minxes. Edward Young's 'On Women', for example, deplores precisely the studied contrariness relished in *The Art*: 'Her lover must be sad, to please her spleen, | His mirth is an inexpiable sin.'[25] Moralists and polemicists often condemned women's partiality to expensive imported luxuries and their tendency towards avarice and extravagance.[26] Collier describes how husbands lavish clothes and all sorts of other vanities upon their wives, agreeing that these blandishments finally breed contempt in women whose reciprocal fondness lasts only as long as the gifts do. Wives' 'coquette-behaviour' (p. 48) is magnified tenfold when they themselves hold the purse strings—when, for example, they have brought their own fortunes to a marriage. On the surface, Collier's description of vain, manipulative wives is remarkably similar to Young's. But behind her mirth and occasional vitriol, unlike those of male satirists, lies an awareness of the many miserable marriages that must have existed in the eighteenth century. Although a wife might have enjoyed an allowance, most of her assets would have passed at her marriage from her father to her husband, and she would have been fully dependent upon him for subsistence and company. Collier's subtext in *The Art* is that women *need* more advice about how to torment others because of their relative powerlessness at home.

Collier makes literary capital out of the boredom which surely afflicted many middle-class women, even those who enjoyed an affluent lifestyle. When gentlewomen could afford to employ domestic help, their workloads were eased by housekeepers, chambermaids, cooks, and nursery staff. Servants' accommodation and clothes were usually provided by their employers, so the more well-dressed servants a family could afford, the stronger the impression they could create of enjoying wealth and prosperity. The leisured middle-class lady, delicate and unsuited to work, herself became a status symbol—and, at the same time, a source

---

[25] Edward Young, *Love of Fame, the Universal Passion. In Seven Characteristicall Satires* (2nd edn., 1728), satire 6, p. 10.

[26] Compare Eliza Haywood's remarks against women's extravagance in dress, entertainment, food, and drink: 'Avarice introduced luxury, luxury leads to contempt, and beggary comes on apace.' Spacks (ed.), *Selections from The Female Spectator*, 48.

of anxiety. Joseph Addison and Richard Steele remarked in the pages of *The Spectator* and *The Tatler* that middle-class women who enjoyed displaying the wealth of their husbands or fathers were becoming as frivolous and demanding as ladies pampered at court, while Fordyce pointed out apprehensively that 'there are many young ladies, whose situation does not supply a sphere of domestic exercise sufficient to fill up that part of their time, which is not necessarily appropriated to female occupations and innocent amusements,' urging them to fill their spare hours purposefully and wisely.[27] Collier suggests mischievously that middle-class women employ their copious spare time experimenting with their increasing levels of authority over servants. The spiteful pleasure some ladies must have taken in abusing these responsibilities is suggested by her proposed techniques for humiliating domestic staff. Mistresses may reject their servants' reasonable excuses and make unreasonable and self-contradictory demands. They may exploit their servants' vulnerability to class-inflected criticism, accusing them of rising impertinently above themselves. A lady may trick a new maid into believing that she is her intimate friend and, in so doing, 'draw her on to a freedom of speech, that, without such encouragement, would never have come into her head'. The maid's forthrightness may then be cruelly punished, for her mistress may 'upbraid her with being sprung from a dunghill' and openly chastise herself for 'conversing with so low a wretch' (p. 19). The best way to subdue the pride of a social inferior, indeed, is to tell her ''twould much better become my station, than yours' (p. 26). The studious efforts ladies make in *The Art* to assert their social superiority suggest the real difficulty some women experienced in exercising authority over domestic staff—and their pressing desire to do so. Once again Collier describes women's faults in order better to expose them; in this case, the shameful, self-serving impulses which lay behind middle-class snobbery, and their cruel effects on the most helpless members of a household.

---

[27] Todd discusses the contribution made by Addison and Steele to this debate in *The Sign of Angellica*, 32. Fordyce, *Sermons to Young Women*, vol. ii, sermon 8, 'On Female Virtue, with Intellectual Accomplishments', 55–6.

The chapter on humble companions explores the business of organized philanthropy with which women were increasingly involved at this time. The dependants Collier describes were often well-educated and well-born women who had fallen on hard times, perhaps because of the death of their parents or other family providers. Collier unmasks the pseudo-compassion which motivated some ladies to invite dependants into their homes, acting not out of a godly desire to help a fellow creature in distress, nor in anticipation of the gratitude they might receive for kindnesses freely bestowed, but to satisfy a longing for 'new subjects of their power' (p. 22). Humble companions were especially vulnerable because, unlike servants, they were unwaged and wholly dependent upon the charity of others.[28] A lady may lavish compliments, sweetmeats, and promises on her companion after abusing her horribly, giving the poor girl the impression that she is herself at fault. She may complain about her companion's very footfalls and, when these are muffled, accuse her of creeping around the house. She may express hollow pity for her companion's imaginary embarrassing foibles (smelly feet, bad breath) clutching smelling salts to her nose whenever she appears. In a twisted inversion of empathy, or what Collier calls 'a fine game at compassion' (p. 33), she may pretend to be a surrogate for the loving parents her dependant has lost and then dash her hopes by suddenly turning cruel. Well versed in the art of verbal abuse, she may pick on a girl's plainness or slowness—or, indeed, her beauty or wit—employing a 'jargon of insult, reproach, and seeming tenderness' (p. 27). Despite her keen awareness of class difference, and her scrutiny of the frustrations caused by women's confinement and isolation, Collier is not advocating reform along the lines of Mary Wollstonecraft's radically emancipatory vision of the 1790s. Her real interest lies in what Judith Hawley has called the 'texture of social exchange'.[29] Focusing on the subtle and often indefinable ways people affect and influence one

---

[28] Bridget Hill discusses female companions, and the class-related unease they created, in *Women Alone*, 62. On the relative status of servants and dependants, see Rizzo, *Companions Without Vows*, 47.

[29] Hawley (ed.), *The Art of Ingeniously Tormenting*, p. xix.

another in a domestic setting, *The Art* explores the possibility that the everyday lives of all members of a household may improve if they treat one another with mutual respect.

The Education of Women

Much of the humour in *The Art* hinges on debates about women's education on which there was little consensus. The ladies' academies and affordable elementary schools for girls, appearing in the early to mid-eighteenth century, had few pedagogical aspirations in the first instance, aiming first and foremost to prepare women from fairly well-to-do families for marriage. But as autodidacticism continued to rise and educational literature began to be published in greater quantities, women found themselves able to benefit professionally and commercially in new ways from education.[30] Teaching was a respectable profession, and many middle-class women made a living as governesses to families who could afford to educate their children at home. Collier addresses her readers as pupils or scholars, and begins *The Art* with a defence of tormenting as an ancient science and a noble art which is useful enough to be taught in 'every nation under heaven' (p. 5). Men and women have displayed over centuries a natural flair for tormenting, but have not yet the arsenal at their disposal to bring its practice to perfection. It is this arsenal which Collier proposes to supply in *The Art*, distinguishing between common, vulgar methods of plaguing others, such as straightforward scolding, and the more refined strokes of the expert tormentor.

Collier would have been familiar with recent and contemporary pedagogical writings. She may have read Locke's *Some Thoughts Concerning Education* (1693) which considers the moral benefits of education, including the role of parental guidance, and stresses the importance of training children to become responsible members of society rather than book-bound scholars. She may also have known Mary Astell's *A Serious Proposal to the Ladies for the Advancement of their True and Greatest Interest*

---

[30] Hill, *Women Alone*, 55; Turner, *Living by the Pen*, 72–3.

(1694) and *A Serious Proposal, Part 2* (1697), both influenced by Locke, which attributed women's errors to 'the mistakes of our Education'. Astell argued that women often fail to achieve godliness because they have been trained to value only vanity, folly, idleness, skittishness, and 'foolish Amours'. She therefore advocated the establishment of academies for women based on principles of spiritual retirement, suggesting that they transfer their attentions from the corruptible realm of the body to the immortal sphere of the mind. Daniel Defoe responded to Astell's *Serious Proposal*, doubting that young ladies could be educated out of their 'natural' tendencies towards levity but arguing that they should nevertheless enjoy 'the advantages of education'.[31] Collier may have encountered the discussion of women's education written by 'Sophia', *Woman not Inferior to Man: or, A short and modest Vindication of the natural Right of the FAIR-SEX* (1739) and, more recently, the fiercely polemical *Beauty's Triumph: Or the Superiority of the Fair Sex, Invincibly Proved* (1751) which argued that women were as capable as men of assimilating history, politics, and philosophy.[32] She was certainly familiar with Sarah Fielding's *The Governess: or, Little Female Academy* (1749), a book designed to teach 'girls how to behave to each other, and to their teachers,' for she is known to have read it in proof.[33] Like many women of her generation, she probably read *The Tatler* and *The Spectator*, as well as satirical responses such as *The Female Spectator*, all of which contained essays on women's education and sought to inform readers as well as entertain them. Haywood published in *The Female Spectator* a letter from 'Cleora' which deplored women's impoverished educational opportunities

[31] Mary Astell, *A Serious Proposal to the Ladies*, ed. Patricia Springborg (London: Pickering and Chatto, 1997), 10. Daniel Defoe, 'An Academy for Women', in *An Essay Upon Projects* (1697). See *The Earlier Life and the Chief Earlier Works of Daniel Defoe*, ed. Henry Morley (London: George Routledge and Sons, 1889), 23–164, at pp. 145–6. Defoe's essay is discussed in Astell, *A Serious Proposal*, ed. Springborg, p. xiii.

[32] *Beauty's Triumph: Or the Superiority of the Fair Sex, Invincibly Proved* (1751), Pt. 3 ('Proving Woman Superior in Excellence to Man'), esp. p. 245.

[33] The quotation appears in Collier's letter to Samuel Richardson, dated 4 October 1748, in which she respectfully requests that *The Governess* be printed without his proposed alterations. See *The Correspondence of Samuel Richardson*, ed. Barbauld, ii. 61–5. Audrey Bilger discusses the implications of the letter in her edition of *The Art*, 13–14.

('Why do [men] call us *silly women*, and not endeavour to make us otherwise?') and argued that the study of philosophy, mathematics, and geography would remedy women's restlessness and inspire them to live virtuous lives. The husbands of educated women would also reap the benefits, she reasoned, for undertaking a purposeful programme of reading would leave wives with less time to pry into their affairs.[34] *The Female Spectator* and Charlotte Lennox's later *Lady's Monthly Museum* (1760–1) both linked friendship, virtue, and intellectual pursuits, anticipating the Bluestocking movement which flourished in the 1770s and 1780s. Their mid-century advances eventually laid the groundwork for Catherine Macaulay's *Letters on Education* (1790) and, especially, Mary Wollstonecraft's trailblazing *A Vindication of the Rights of Woman* (1792).[35]

At the same time, however, the educated woman became a figure of hatred and suspicion. Polemicists and satirists quoted 1 Timothy 1: 12–13: 'I do not permit a woman to be a teacher, nor must woman domineer over man; she should be quiet.' Some argued that women were easily distracted or corrupted by reading and were drawn towards impure subject matter—especially novels. Molière's play *Les Femmes Savantes* (1672) launched an assault against bookish ladies and was followed by an English comedy, *The Female Wits* (1704), which made fun of women playwrights. The extravagantly literary Phoebe Clinket in *Three Hours After Marriage* (1717), a comedy by John Gay, Alexander Pope, and John Arbuthnot, and the learned figure of Narcissa's aunt in Tobias Smollett's *The Adventures of Roderick Random* (1748), are both figures of ridicule.[36] Perhaps because Restoration prostitutes had been regarded as notoriously witty,

[34] Spacks (ed.), *Selections from The Female Spectator*, 123–38, at p. 123.

[35] Sylvia Harcstark Myers, *The Bluestocking Circle: Women, Friendship, and the Life of the Mind in Eighteenth-Century England* (Oxford: Clarendon Press, 1990), 11. Felicity Nussbaum argues that the mid-eighteenth century heralded an 'inaugural moment for the celebration of a national female genius'. See 'Effeminacy and Femininity: Domestic Prose Satire and *David Simple*', *Eighteenth-Century Fiction*, 11/4 (1999), 421–44, at p. 426.

[36] These examples are discussed in Myers, *The Bluestocking Circle*, 3–4. See also Todd, *The Sign of Angellica*, 118–20; and Hill's chapter on 'Spinsters and Learned Ladies', *Women Alone*, 81–93.

sharp-tongued women were denounced not merely as eccentric but also as morally and sexually tainted. One prominent Blue-stocking, Elizabeth Montagu, argued that 'wit is a dangerous quality . . . like a sword without a scabbard it wounds the wearer, and provokes assailants. I am sorry to say the generality of women who have excelled in wit have failed in chastity.'[37]

Collier draws on both the educational initiatives of her contemporaries and the fears of anti-educationalists and, in so doing, sheds light on both. Her decision to structure *The Art* as a pedagogical treatise is a riposte to those who believed women scarcely capable of reason and their intellects not worth edu-cating. At the same time, however, Collier roguishly unpicks Haywood's confident assertion 'that knowledge can make the bad no worse' in order to reveal the speciousness at the heart of the anti-feminist argument that educating women only makes them more ignorant.[38] *The Art* takes dark delight in demonstrating just how pernicious the consequences might be of schooling ladies who have already proved themselves excellent students of obnox-iousness. Even simple-minded obtuseness is a skill well worth mastering. If your husband wants you to read poetry, 'you may say, that indeed you have other things to mind besides poetry; and if he was uneasy at your taking care of your family and children, and mending *his* shirts, you wished he had a learned wife; and then he would soon see himself in a jail, and his family in rags' (p. 56). Here Collier mocks the damaging assumption that edu-cated women make neglectful wives, incapable of keeping house and fulfilling other domestic responsibilities. The ability sarcas-tically to deride other women's learning also pays dividends. If your sisters-in-law should dare to point out a fine painting during a trip to Windsor Castle, 'you may say "that, indeed, you don't pretend to understand painting and history, and such *learned* things; you leave those studies to such *wise* ladies as they are . . ." ' (pp. 90–1). A dependant makes excellent fodder for teasing if she is well educated, for the tormentor may unleash

[37] Quoted in Todd, *The Sign of Angellica*, 131, from *The Letters of Mrs Elizabeth Montagu*, ed. Matthew Montagu, 4 vols. (London, 1809–13), iii. 96–7.

[38] Spacks (ed.), *Selections from The Female Spectator*, 135.

against her a volley of the well-worn clichés peddled by those who opposed the education of women:

Omit not any of those trite observations; that all *Wits* are slatterns;—that no girl ever delighted in reading, that was not a slut;—that well might the men say they would not for the world marry a *Wit*; that they had rather have a woman who could make a pudden, than one who could make a poem;—and that it was the ruin of all girls who had not independent fortunes, to have learnt either to read or write. (p. 29)

By teaching her students to parrot the most dim-witted arguments of anti-educationalists, particularly the idea that knowledge turns women into sluts, Collier takes a back-handed swipe at their misogyny and lack of imagination.

Women would have assumed much of the responsibility for educating their children to become young adults and, in the chapter of *The Art* addressed to parents, Collier describes how the best tormentors tutor their children from infancy to be a menace to themselves and everyone around them. Collier directs her instructions not towards those who feel 'natural affection and tenderness' (p. 35) towards their offspring, but rather towards those who are willing to exercise irresponsibly the powerful authority conferred by parenthood. The most efficient way of tormenting children, and of turning them into apprentice tormentors in their own right, is to spoil them rotten. Allestree had warned that 'The will of a tender Infant, is like its Limbs, supple and pliant, but time confirms it, and custom hardens it; so 'tis a cruel Indulgence to the poor Creature, to let it contract such habits, which must cost him so dear the breaking.'[39] Collier advises on the contrary that mothers should cram rich food down their children's throats, allow them to stay up late, and (best of all) train them to annoy teatime visitors by sticking snotty noses into the cream pot, drooling into the sugar, and stuffing bread and butter down ladies' backs. Any form of discipline is expressly forbidden, except for the most trifling offences. But behind her

[39] Allestree, *The Ladies Calling*, 193.

triumphant celebration of disruptive behaviour, Collier seems
certain that children are as capable of being properly educated as
they are of being turned by their parents into brats. The stories in
Sarah Fielding's *The Governess*, one of the first books written
expressly for children, were intended to teach little girls 'that
their true interest is concerned in cherishing and improving . . .
amiable dispositions into habits; and in keeping down all rough
and boisterous passions'.[40] Like Fielding, Collier believed the
foundation of children's errors—and the seeds of their potential
usefulness as young citizens—were set down during their earliest
experiences of education.

   Given Collier's feisty contribution to the debate about
learned women, and her shrewd remarks about teaching children, we should take with a pinch of salt the remarks she made
with Sarah Fielding in a letter they wrote in 1751 to James
Harris, a member of the Fieldings' circle who may have helped
Collier draft *The Art*. Here Collier and Fielding quote from
Alexander Pope's 1711 *An Essay on Criticism* ('a little learning
is a dang'rous thing'), describing themselves as 'little children'
who fear 'the censure cast on those women who, having picked
up a few scraps of Horace, immediately imagine themselves
fraught with all knowledge'.[41] But Collier deployed in *The Art*
her knowledge of Horace and many other writers with con-
summate skill. Like many other educated women, especially
those in insecure social circumstances, she must surely have
feared that she might be ridiculed for her wit. But she showed
herself capable in *The Art* of reflecting intelligently on precisely those fears, and of writing with verve and humour about
them.

[40] Sarah Fielding, *The Governess; Or, Little Female Academy* (1749), p. iii.
[41] *The Correspondence of Henry and Sarah Fielding* ed. Martin C. Battestin and
Clive T. Probyn (Oxford: Clarendon Press, 1993), 125. Quoted in Bilger, *The Art*, 13.
The quotation from Pope comes from *An Essay on Criticism*, l. 215. James Harris read
The Art in manuscript and supplied an unused dedication; see Battestin and Battestin,
Henry Fielding, A Life, 665 n. 218.

The Satirical Tradition

Collier's familiarity with classical and contemporary satires informs and enlivens her own satirical voice in *The Art*. Her commonplace book confirms that both Jane and her sister Margaret, who transcribed its contents, knew Latin and Greek—skills foundational to the education of gentlemen but seldom taught to girls because they were thought to be irrelevant to domestic life. She quotes in *The Art* from Abraham Cowley's translation of the works of Martial, the Roman satirical epigrammist, and probably knew Horace's satires as well as *Ars Poetica* before Henry Fielding presented her with a copy of Horace's works in 1754. She may also have had in mind Ovid's *Remedia Amoris*, a poem which supplied antidotes to the fond feelings of men and women for one another.[42] Like most satires, *The Art* exposes human errors with a view towards mending them. Writing about the erosion of family life, Haywood argued that 'Times like these require corrosives, not balsams to amend:—The sore has already eaten into the very bowels of public happiness, and they must tear away the infected part, or become a nuisance to themselves and all about them.'[43] Collier took this challenge seriously and found the corrosive, uncompromising voice of satire perfectly suited to her purpose. *The Art* lays bare the subtly damaging, accumulative effects of petty selfishnesses, especially those indulged by women, in order that families and acquaintances might recognize and eventually change for the better their own lives and those of their loved ones. While Collier protests against the idea that women should be modest and only rudimentarily educated, her satirical voice attacks at the same time the ways in which women stoop to manipulate those around them, indulging precisely the weaknesses for which they are most often criticized. Their malevolent

[42] Fielding inscription to Collier in the copy of Horace praises 'an Understanding more than Female, mixed with virtues almost more than human'. See Battestin and Battestin, *Henry Fielding, A Life*, 393–4; and *The Correspondence of Henry and Sarah Fielding*, ed. Battestin and Probyn, 124 n. 1. Collier's debt to Ovid is discussed by Timothy Dykstal, 'Provoking the Ancients: Classical Learning and Imitation in Fielding and Collier', *College Literature*, 31/3 (2004), 102–22 (esp. pp. 115–17).

[43] Spacks (ed.), *Selections from The Female Spectator*, 48.

acts are moreover seldom punished because they are so carefully tailored to fit in with cultural assumptions about femininity. By conforming to type, Collier suggests, women nourish and sustain the injustices perpetrated against them instead of confronting them directly.

Satire flourished in the Restoration and the eighteenth century as John Dryden, John Wilmot Earl of Rochester, Swift, Pope, and Samuel Johnson developed afresh the heroic intellectual tradition. Women had always been a popular satirical target, but men were directing more vitriol than ever against them in this period. Many criticized not simply women's failings but the 'natural' flaws of the female sex, especially sexual corruption, capriciousness, and narcissism. Swift satirized proud, vain women in 'A Beautiful Young Nymph Going to Bed' where the superficially polished Corinna returns home from London's red-light district, Drury Lane, to pluck off her wig, pop out her artificial eye, unlace her 'steel-ribb'd bodice', and cover her running sores with plasters.[44] In his essay 'A Discourse Concerning the Original and Progress of Satire', Dryden suggested that satire's principle function was to caution readers 'against one particular vice or folly'. Although he distanced himself from the most vicious parts of Juvenal's sixth satire ('Whatever his Roman ladies were, the English are free from all his imputations'), his 1693 translation pillories women who have eclipsed plain simple manners with 'pride, laziness, and all luxurious arts'. Some of the harshest invective is reserved for those who are over-educated:

> But of all plagues, the greatest is untold;
> The book-learned wife, in Greek and Latin bold[45]

---

[44] Jonathan Swift, *Major Works*, ed. Angus Ross and David Woolley (Oxford: Oxford World's Classics, 1984), 533–4, l. 24. For a discussion of Pope and Swift's satires against women, see Felicity Nussbaum, *The Brink of All We Hate: English Satires on Women, 1660–1750* (Lexington: University Press of Kentucky, 1984), esp. ch. 6.

[45] John Dryden, *The Major Works*, ed. Keith Walker (Oxford: Oxford University Press, 1987; repr. Oxford World's Classics, 2003), 336–58, ll. 416 and 575–6. The quotation from Dryden's essay is found in *Essays of John Dryden*, ed. W. P. Ker, 2 vols. (New York: Russell & Russell, 1961), ii. 102.

Writing along the same lines, and with typical hyperbole, Young warned women to 'Beware the fever of the mind':

> Is't not enough plagues, wars, and famines rise
> To lash our crimes, but must our wives be *wise*?

George Lyttelton agreed in *Advice to a Lady*, cautioning women to

> wisely rest content with modest sense;
> For wit, like wine, intoxicates the brain,
> Too strong for feeble woman to sustain[46]

Pope refined these nightmarish visions of female wit in *An Epistle to a Lady*, praising the modest, cultured intelligence of the poem's dedicatee, Martha Blount, in comparison to Philomedé who foolishly flaunts her learning by 'lecturing all mankind'. And in an issue of *The Spectator* published in 1711, Abraham Thrifty complains about his over-educated nieces: 'Whilst they should have been considering the proper ingredients for a sack-posset, you should hear a dispute concerning the magnetical virtue of the loadstone, or perhaps the pressure of the atmosphere.'[47] Whether they are describing negligent wives and mothers, vain coquettes, or alarmingly articulate scholars, these satires share an anxiety about women's moral imperfections. Collier's purposes were very different, but she may have drawn from her contemporaries some ideas for turning abuse into a finely honed art.

Satire's characteristically combative, assertive wit meant that it was an essentially masculine genre, and female satirists were often regarded by men as both threatening and unnatural. Fordyce warned young ladies that 'an air and deportment, of the masculine kind, are always forbidding' and this held as true in print as it

---

[46] Young, *Love of Fame*, satire V, pp. 26 and 5. George Lyttelton, *Advice to a Lady* (1733), 5.

[47] Alexander Pope, 'An Epistle to a Lady. Of the Characters of Women', in Alexander Pope, *Selected Poetry*, ed. Pat Rogers (Oxford: Oxford University Press, 1994; repr. Oxford World's Classics, 1998), 108, l. 83. Donald F. Bond (ed.), *The Spectator*, 5 vols. (Oxford: Clarendon Press, 1965; reissued 1987), ii. 442: no. 242 (7 December 1711).

did in everyday life.[48] Pope's witty woman, Atossa, suggests the perils women exposed themselves to when they criticized others, for although she

> Shines, in exposing knaves, and painting fools,
> Yet is, whate'er she hates and ridicules
> . . .
> So much the fury still outran the wit,
> The pleasure missed her, and the scandal hit.[49]

Outspoken, articulate women, particularly those who criticized others in print, sometimes received far more savage treatment than the targets of their own satires. Collier risked being compared to the shrewish women she so eloquently lampooned, and it is easy to underestimate the extent to which she laid herself open to reproach. It was not long since the satirical novelist Delarivière Manley (1663–1724) had been denounced for publishing material related to her scandalous life, and it is telling that some of Collier's first readers assumed that *The Art* was written by a man— although Collier joked that 'My being the author is now one of those profound secrets that is known only to all the people that I know.' Lady Mary Wortley Montagu assumed that it was by Sarah Fielding; her underwhelmed response, preserved in a letter to her daughter, was that it 'tormented me very much'.[50] The unsuitability of satire as a genre for women writers is suggested in the 1804 edition of *The Art*, where Jane's brother Arthur is recorded as having lamented 'that a sister possessing such amiable manners, and such abilities, should only be known to the literary world by a satirical work'.[51] The unique interest of *The Art* lies not

[48] Fordyce, *Sermons to Young Women*, vol. ii, sermon 12, 'On Female Meekness', 265.

[49] Pope, 'An Epistle to a Lady. Of the Characters of Women', 109, ll. 119–28.

[50] An extract from *The Art* was printed in *The Monthly Review*, 8 (April 1753), 274–81. The reviewer was unenthusiastic: 'tho' no extraordinary genius for satyr appears in it, it is far from being a contemptible performance' (p. 274). *The Complete Letters of Lady Mary Wortley Montagu*, ed. Robert Halsband, 3 vols. (Oxford: Clarendon Press, 1965–7), iii. 88. Collier's joke appears in a letter to James Harris, found in *The Correspondence of Henry and Sarah Fielding*, ed. Battestin and Probyn, p. xxxiii n. 38.

[51] 'Advertisement of the Present Editor' in the prefatory material to *The Art* (1804).

only in its subtly outraged response to protocols of modest, refined femininity, but also to the assumption that women could not or should not write satire.

Collier's very first satirical examples deal not with domestic scenes but issues affecting society at large. Perhaps she was drawing from her family's own bitter experience when she suggests that the fiscal and legal linchpins of society must surely have been carefully designed to torment those least able to defend themselves. Debtors who lack only the means and not the will to pay make excellent victims for the tormentor whose voice Collier adroitly assumes: 'I instantly throw him into jail, and there I keep him to pine away his life in want and misery' (p. 8). The tormentor's sport is doubled if the wretched man has a wife and children to support, and trebled if he is finally driven insane by his plight. Collier draws her reader into complicitous agreement, suggesting that the pleasures of tormenting are their own reward even if no money is recovered: 'You mistake greatly, my friend, if you think I defeat my own ends;—for my ends are to plague and torment, not only a fellow creature, but a fellow Christian' (p. 8). Collier cajoles us into imitating her outrageous behaviour and, at the same time, exposes our unchristian cruelty. One of her main achievements as a satirist is her ability to manipulate her own voice: by cleverly ventriloquizing arguments she disagrees with, she hands over to her readers the responsibility to arbitrate the debate.

Collier's closing parable further illuminates the purposes of her satire. In a mythical past age, she writes, the lion, the leopard, and the lynx squabbled bitterly over whose ancestors had written an old poem signed only with the letter 'L' describing the 'exquisite torment' (p. 100) felt by prey when their living flesh is torn apart. Only the horse guesses the true identity of the author:

'For it is impossible', says he, 'that any beast, that has the feeling which our author shows for the tortured wretches who are torn by savage teeth and claws, should ever make the ravages, which, it is notorious, are daily made by the three fierce competitors before us. The writer of this poem, therefore,' continued he, 'must be no other than the lamb. As it is from suffering, and not from inflicting torments, that the true idea of them is gained.' (p. 100)

It is only possible to write about torment, in other words, if one has first been tormented. The parable neatly encapsulates two possible responses to *The Art*. Whereas a frivolous reader will merely enjoy Collier's wit, mistaking her voice for those of the tormentors she lampoons, a more sympathetic reader will register her subtle and sometimes poignant defence of society's most vulnerable groups.[52] For although *The Art* is a conventional satire insofar as it exposes the faults of wrongdoers with a view towards reforming them, its other important accomplishment is to express allegiance with tormentors' long-suffering victims. If Collier's voice at times seems strident, it is so that we may better hear the voiceless.

[52] Audrey Bilger, *Laughing Feminism: Subversive Comedy in Frances Burney, Maria Edgeworth, and Jane Austen* (Detroit: Wayne State University Press, 1998), 196.

NOTE ON THE TEXT

THE present text is based on the second London edition of *An Essay on the Art of Ingeniously Tormenting*, published in octavo by Andrew Millar in 1757. Collier died before this edition appeared in print but it seems likely that she at least had a hand in revising the first edition of 1753 which was printed for Millar by Samuel Richardson. The 1757 edition contains a new 'Advertisement to the Reader' consistent in tone with the rest of *The Art* and other light revisions, especially the addition of quotation marks and paragraph breaks. A Dublin edition appeared in the same year as the first London printing, and subsequent editions were published in 1795, 1804, 1805, 1806, 1808, 1809, and 1811. Significant variations between the first and second London editions are recorded in the Explanatory Notes.

The text was prepared using one of the two copies of *The Art* held in the Bodleian Library, Oxford (26520.e.63) and has been lightly modernized throughout. Collier's rhetorical style often results in long sentences made up of clauses separated by commas, colons, and semicolons. Punctuation has been regularized only where the original may present difficulty to the modern reader. Spelling has been modernized only in words whose sense is unaffected, and paragraph breaks remain unaltered. Initial capital letters used for emphasis have been retained, but when Collier capitalizes a whole word for emphasis this has been changed to italics. Obvious errors of typography have been silently corrected. Like her friend Sarah Fielding, Collier often employs a series of short dashes, especially in direct speech. These have been replaced in this edition by one long dash. When Collier has added a footnote, this appears in the text as a superior numerical figure; asterisks refer to the Explanatory Notes.

SELECT BIBLIOGRAPHY

Original Editions

An Essay on the Art of Ingeniously Tormenting; With Proper Rules for the Exercise of that Pleasant Art (London: printed for Andrew Millar, 1753).

An Essay on the Art of Ingeniously Tormenting; With Proper Rules for the Exercise of that Pleasant Art (Dublin: printed for John Smith, Peter Wilson, John Exshaw, and Matthew Williamson, 1753).

An Essay on the Art of Ingeniously Tormenting; With Proper Rules for the Exercise of that Pleasant Art . . . The Second Edition, Corrected (London: printed for Andrew Millar, 1757).

An Essay on the Art of Ingeniously Tormenting: A New Edition (London: printed for Allen & West; York: Wilson, Spence and Mawman; and Edinburgh: J. Mundell and Co., 1795).

An Essay on the Art of Ingeniously Tormenting: with Proper Rules for the Exercise of that Amusing Study (London: reprinted for William Miller in Old Bond Street, 1804).

An Essay on the Art of Ingeniously Tormenting: with Proper Rules for the Exercise of that Amusing Study (London: reprinted for William Miller in Albermarle Street by W. Bulmer and Co., Cleveland Row, 1805).

An Essay on the Art of Ingeniously Tormenting: with Proper Rules for the Exercise of that Amusing Study (London: printed for Andrew Millar, 1806).

An Essay on the Art of Ingeniously Tormenting (London: printed for Thomas Tegg by Hazard and Carthew, 1808).

An Essay on the Art of Ingeniously Tormenting (London: printed for Thomas Tegg and R. Scholey, 1809).

An Essay on the Art of Ingeniously Tormenting: with Proper Rules for the Exercise of that Amusing Study (London: printed for William Miller and James Ballantyne, 1811).

Modern Editions

Judith Hawley (ed.), *The Art of Ingeniously Tormenting* (Bristol: Thoemmes Press, 1994): facsimile of 1757 edition.

Audrey Bilger (ed.), *An Essay on the Art of Ingeniously Tormenting*

(Peterborough, Ont.: Broadview Press, 2003): 1753 edition in old spelling.

General Criticism

Armstrong, Nancy, and Tennenhouse, Leonard (eds.), *The Ideology of Conduct: Essays on Literature and the History of Sexuality* (New York and London: Methuen, 1987).

Ballaster, Rosalind, 'Manl(e)y Forms: Sex and the Female Satirist', in Clare Brant and Diane Purkiss (eds.), *Women, Texts and Histories, 1575–1760* (London: Routledge, 1992), 217–41.

Bilger, Audrey, *Laughing Feminism: Subversive Comedy in Frances Burney, Maria Edgeworth, and Jane Austen* (Detroit: Wayne State University Press, 1998).

Brissenden, R. F., *Virtue in Distress: Studies in the Novel of Sentiment from Richardson to Sade* (London: Macmillan, 1974).

Gordon, Scott Paul, *The Power of the Passive Self in English Literature, 1640–1770* (Cambridge: Cambridge University Press, 2002).

Hill, Bridget, *Women Alone: Spinsters in England, 1660–1850* (New Haven and London: Yale University Press, 2001).

Jones, Vivien (ed.), *Women in the Eighteenth Century: Constructions of Femininity* (London: Routledge, 1990).

Myers, Sylvia Harcstark, *The Bluestocking Circle: Women, Friendship, and the Life of the Mind in Eighteenth-Century England* (Oxford: Clarendon Press, 1990).

Nussbaum, Felicity A., *The Brink of All We Hate: English Satires on Women, 1660–1750* (Lexington: University Press of Kentucky, 1984).

Rizzo, Betty, *Companions Without Vows: Relationships among Eighteenth-Century British Women* (Athens, Ga. and London: University of Georgia Press, 1994).

Todd, Janet, *The Sign of Angellica: Women, Writing, and Fiction, 1660–1800* (London: Virago, 1989).

—— *Sensibility: An Introduction* (London: Methuen, 1986).

Turner, Cheryl, *Living by the Pen: Women Writers in the Eighteenth Century* (London: Routledge, 1992).

Yeazell, Ruth Bernard, *Fictions of Modesty: Women and Courtship in the English Novel* (Chicago and London: University of Chicago Press, 1991).

Collier and her Contemporaries

Barchas, Janine, 'Sarah Fielding's Dashing Style and Eighteenth-Century Print Culture', *English Literary History*, 63/3 (1996), 633–56.

Battestin, Martin C. with Battestin, Ruthe R., *Henry Fielding, A Life* (London: Routledge, 1989; repr. 1993).

De Castro, J. Paul, 'Fielding and the Collier Family', *Notes and Queries*, 12/2 (1916), 104–6.

—— 'Henry Fielding's Last Voyage', *The Library*, 3/8 (1917), 145–59.

—— 'A Presentation Inscription by Fielding', *Notes and Queries*, 178 (1940), 337–9.

Dykstal, Timothy, 'Provoking the Ancients: Classical Learning and Imitation in Fielding and Collier', *College Literature*, 31/3 (2004), 102–22.

Eaves, T. C. Duncan, and Kimpel, Ben D., *Samuel Richardson: A Biography* (Oxford: Clarendon Press, 1971).

Fielding, Henry and Sarah, *The Correspondence of Henry and Sarah Fielding*, ed. Martin C. Battestin and Clive T. Probyn (Oxford: Clarendon Press, 1993).

Grundy, Isobel, 'Jane Collier', in *The New Oxford Dictionary of National Biography*.

Haywood, Eliza, *Selections from The Female Spectator*, ed. Patricia Meyer Spacks (Oxford: Oxford University Press, 1999).

Keymer, Tom, 'Jane Collier, Reader of Richardson, and the Fire Scene in *Clarissa*', in Albert J. Rivero (ed.), *New Essays on Samuel Richardson* (Basingstoke: Macmillan, 1996), 141–61.

Londry, Michael, 'Our Dear Miss Jenny Collier', *TLS* (5 March 2004), 13–14.

Nussbaum, Felicity, 'Effeminacy and Femininity: Domestic Prose Satire and *David Simple*', *Eighteenth-Century Fiction*, 11/4 (1999), 421–44.

Richardson, Samuel, *The Correspondence of Samuel Richardson*, ed. Anna Laetitia Barbauld, 6 vols. (London: Richard Phillips, 1804).

Woodward, Carolyn, 'Who Wrote *The Cry*?: A Fable for Our Times', *Eighteenth-Century Fiction*, 9/1 (1996), 91–7.

Further Reading in Oxford World's Classics

Austen, Jane, *Persuasion*, ed. Claudia Johnson and James Kinsley.

Burney, Frances, *Evelina*, ed. Vivien Jones and Edward A. Bloom.

Dryden, John, *The Major Works*, ed. Keith Walker.
Fielding, Henry, *Tom Jones*, ed. John Bender and Simon Stern.
Pope, Alexander, *Selected Poetry*, ed. Pat Rogers.
Richardson, Samuel, *Pamela*, ed. Thomas Keymer and Alice Wakely.
Swift, Jonathan, *Major Works*, ed. Angus Ross and David Woolley.

A CHRONOLOGY OF JANE COLLIER

1715   (16 Jan.) Jane Collier christened at Langford Magna (now Steeple Langford) in Wiltshire, the daughter of the philosopher and clergyman, the Reverend Arthur Collier, and Margaret Johnson.

1716   Collier family move to Salisbury because of financial difficulties.

1726   Swift, *Gulliver's Travels*.

1727   George I succeeded by George II.

1732   Death of the Reverend Arthur Collier.

1739–40 Hume, *Treatise of Human Nature*.

1744   Sarah Fielding, *The Adventures of David Simple*.

1747   Sarah Fielding, *Familiar Letters between the Principal Characters in David Simple*.

Late 1740s JC meets Samuel Richardson and later lives with his family as a companion and friend.

1747–8 Richardson, *Clarissa*.

1748 or 1749 JC moves to her brother Arthur's lodgings at the ecclesiastical court of Doctors' Commons in London.

1749   Death of Margaret Johnson. JC writes a short essay praising Richardson's *Clarissa*, originally intended for publication in *The Gentleman's Magazine*. Sarah Fielding, *The Governess*; JC corrects the proofs.

        Henry Fielding, *Tom Jones*.

1750   Richardson presents JC with a copy of *Meditations . . . Being Those Mentioned in the History of Clarissa*.

1751   JC probably living with Sarah Fielding in Beauford Buildings, Westminster.

1753   (Mar.) *An Essay on The Art of Ingeniously Tormenting* printed by Samuel Richardson and published in London by Andrew Millar; a separate Dublin edition appears the same year. Sarah Fielding, *The Adventures of David Simple, Volume the Last*, with a preface probably by JC

Henry Fielding presents JC with a copy of Horace's *Works*. (1 July) JC accompanies her sister Margaret to Gravesend on the first stage of her journey with Henry Fielding's party to Portugal. Publication of *The Cry: a New Dramatic Fable*, co-authored with Sarah Fielding.

1755   Death of JC. Buried on 28 March in London at St Benet Paul's Wharf, Doctors' Commons. Johnson cites JC's *The Art* in his *Dictionary*.

1757   Second London edition of *An Essay on The Art of Ingeniously Tormenting*.

AN
ESSAY

ON THE

ART of *ingeniously* TORMENTING;

WITH

PROPER RULES

FOR

The EXERCISE of that Pleasant ART.

Humbly addressed,

In the First Part,	In the Second Part,
To the { MASTER, HUSBAND, &c.	To the { WIFE, FRIEND, &c.

With some GENERAL INSTRUCTIONS for
Plaguing all your Acquaintance.

——*Speak Daggers*——*but use none.*
SHAKESPEARE.

The SECOND EDITION, Corrected.

LONDON:
Printed for A. MILLAR, in the Strand.
M.DCC.LVII.

CELEBRARE DOMESTICA FACTA.

The Cat doth play,
And after slay. *Childs Guide*

ADVERTISEMENT TO THE READER*

As it cannot be supposed, that people buy the rules of any science in which they are already proficients, the sale of our first impression of this most useful treatise is at least a presumptive proof of our being in the right, when we asserted that mankind were not so thoroughly perfect in the ingenious art we endeavour to teach as was insinuated by a discourager of this our undertaking; and is therefore one good reason why we present the public with a second.

'Tis generally thought necessary with a new edition of any book to publish some additions; but the apology of the author for deviating from this practice is really and truly no other than her not having anything material to add, which she can believe would be acceptable. The simple precept she was taught by her parents, that 'when she had nothing to say, she should say nothing,' is so deeply impressed on her mind, that she has ever endeavoured to make it the rule of her conversation: And how many trifling performances would this rule prevent from appearing in public, did authors likewise remember, that when they had nothing to write, they modestly should write nothing.

A collection of the letters which an author receives on the first publication, often makes a very splendid figure at the beginning of a second impression: But the good nature and universal benevolence of mankind is so great, that they generally attribute such performances to the author himself; and he has no way of preventing an honour being thus forced on him, but by declining to publish such letters. For fear therefore of receiving praises for wit or humour which is not her own, our author of *The Art of Tormenting* is resolved to publish no such testimonies, nor to plead any other approbation of her essay, or encouragement for the publication of this second edition, than by saying, that the bookseller assures her, that there are not any of the first left; and that it is much enquired after.

AN
ESSAY
ON THE
Art *of* Tormenting

 NGLAND has ever been allowed to excel most other nations in her improvements of arts and sciences, although she seldom claims to herself the merit of invention: to her improvements also are many of her neighbours indebted, for the exercise of some of their most useful arts.

'Tis not the benefit that may arise to the few from any invention, but its general utility, which ought to make such invention of universal estimation. Had the art of navigation gone no higher than to direct the course of a small boat by oars, the Low Countries* only could have been the better for it. Again, should the inhabitants of Lapland invent the most convenient method for warming their houses by stoves, bringing them, by their improvements, to the utmost perfection; yet could not those who live within the Tropics receive the least benefit from such their improvements; any more than the Laplanders could, from the invention of fans, umbrellas, and cooling grottos.

But as the science recommended in this short essay will be liable to no such exceptions; being, we presume, adapted to the circumstances, genius, and capacity of every nation under heaven, why should I doubt of that deserved fame, generally given to those

> *Inventas aut qui vitam excoluere per artes,*
> *Quique sui memores alios fecere merendo?**
>
> Virgil, *Æneid*, vi. 663–4

Unless, indeed, I should be told, that mankind are already too great adepts in this art, to need any farther instructions.

May I hope that my dear countrymen will pardon me for presuming (by the very publication of these rules) that they are not already absolutely perfect in this our science? Or at least, that they may not always have an ingenious Torment ready at hand to inflict?

By the common run of servants, it might have been presumed that Dean Swift's instructions* to them were unnecessary: but I dare believe no one ever read over that ingenious work, without finding there some inventions for idleness, carelessness, and ill-behaviour, which had never happened within his own experience.

Although I do not suppose mankind in general to be thorough proficients in this our art; yet wrong not my judgement so much, gentle reader, as to imagine that I would write *institutes** of any science, to those who are unqualified for its practice, or do not show some genius in themselves towards it. Should you observe in one child a delight of drawing, in another a turn towards music, would you not do your utmost to assist their genius, and to further their attempts? 'Tis the great progress that I have observed to be already made in this our pleasant art, and the various attempts that I daily see towards bringing it to perfection, that encouraged me to offer this my poor assistance.

One requisite for approbation I confess is wanting in this work; for, alas! I fear it will contain nothing new. But what is wanting in novelty, shall be made up in utility; for, although I may not be able to show one new and untried method of plaguing, teasing, or tormenting; yet will it not be a very great help to anyone, to have all the best and most approved methods collected together, in one small pocket volume? Did I promise a new set of rules, then, whatever was not mine, might be claimed by its proper owner; and, like the jay in the fable,* I should justly be stripped of my borrowed plumes: but, as I declare myself only a humble collector, I doubt not, but everyone who has practised, or who in writing has described, an ingenious Torment, will thank me for putting it into this my curious collection.

That a love to this science is implanted in our natures, or early inculcated, is very evident, from the delight many children take in teasing and tormenting little dogs, cats, squirrels, or any other harmless animal, that they get into their power.

This love of Tormenting may be said to have one thing in common with what, some writers affirm, belongs to the true love of virtue; namely, that it is exercised for its own sake, and no other: For, can there be a clearer proof, that, for its own sake alone, this art of Tormenting is practised, than that it never did, nor ever can, answer any other end? I know that the most expert practitioners deny this; and frequently declare, when they whip, cut, and slash the body, or when they tease, vex, and torment the mind, that 'tis done for the good of the person that suffers. Let the vulgar believe this if they will; but I, and my good pupils, understand things better; and, while we can enjoy the high pleasure of Tormenting, it matters not what the objects of our power either feel, think, or believe.

With what contempt may we, adepts in this science, look down on the tyrants of old! On Nero, Caligula, Phalaris,* and all such paltry pretenders to our art! Their inventions ending in death, freed the sufferer from any farther Torments; or, if they extended only to broken bones, and bodily wounds, they were such as the skill of the surgeon could rectify, or heal: But where is the hand can cure the wounds of unkindness, which our ingenious artists inflict?

The practice of tormenting the body is not now, indeed, much allowed, except in some particular countries, where slavery and ignorance subsist: but let us not, my dear countrymen, regret the loss of that trifling branch of our power, since we are at full liberty to exercise ourselves in that much higher pleasure, the tormenting the mind. Nay, the very laws themselves, although they restrain us from being too free with our bastinado,* pay so much regard to this our strong desire of Tormenting, that, in some instances, they give us the fairest opportunities we could wish, of legally indulging ourselves in this pleasant sport.

To make myself clearly understood, examine the case, as it stands (if I mistake not) between the debtor and creditor.

If a person owes me a thousand pounds (which perhaps, too, may be my all), and has an estate of yearly that value, he may, if he pleases, and has a mind to plague, distress, and vex me, refuse paying me my money. 'Arrest him, then,' cry you.—If he be not in parliament, I do.*—He gives bail; and, with my own money, works me through all the quirks of the law.—At last (if he be of the true blood of those my best disciples, who would hang themselves to spite their neighbours) he retires into the liberties of the Fleet, or King's Bench;* lives at his ease, and laughs at me and my family, who are starving. However, as some inconveniences attend such a proceeding, this method of plaguing a creditor is not very often practised.

But on the other hand, how can I be thankful enough to our good laws, for indulging me in the pleasure of persecuting and tormenting a man who is indebted to me, and who does not want the *will*, but the *power*, to pay me!

As soon as I perceive this to be the case, I instantly throw him into jail, and there I keep him to pine away his life in want and misery.—How will my pleasure be increased, if he should be a man in any business or profession! For I then rob him of all probable means of escaping my power. It may be objected, perhaps, that in this last instance I act imprudently; that I defeat my own ends, and am myself the means of my losing my whole money.—How ignorant of the true joys of Tormenting is such an objector! You mistake greatly, my friend, if you think I defeat my own ends;—for my ends are to plague and torment, not only a fellow creature but a fellow Christian.—And are there not instances enough of this kind of practice, to make us fairly suppose, that the value of one thousand, or ten thousand pounds, is nothing, compared to the excessive delight of Tormenting?

But let me raise this joyous picture a little higher.—Must not my sport be doubled and trebled by the consideration, that his children are starving; that his wife is in the same condition, oppressed also with unspeakable anguish for not being able to give her helpless infants any relief?—Suppose, too, that the husband, with the reflection of all this, and his own incapacity to help them, should be driven to distraction! Would not this exceed the most malicious transports of revenge ever exercised by an ancient or modern tyrant?

If there are some odd sort of people, who have no great relish for this kind of pleasure,* which I have here attempted to describe; yet let them not hastily condemn it, as unnatural: for I appeal to the experience of mankind; and ask—whether there is anyone who has not heard of, at least, one instance of distress, near as high as the scene before described? And that the love of Tormenting must have been the sole motive to a creditor's acting in such a manner, when his debtor could not pay him, is evident, from the impossibility of reasonably assigning any other cause.

One strong objection, I know, will be made against my whole design, by people of weak consciences; which is, that every rule I shall lay down will be exactly opposite to the doctrine of Christianity. Greatly, indeed, in a Christian country, should I fear the force of such an objection, could I perceive, that any one vice was refrained from on that account only. Both theft and murder are forbidden by God himself: yet can anyone say, that our lives and properties would be in the least secure, were it not for the penal laws of our country? Who is there, that having received a blow on one cheek, will turn the other,* while revenge can be had from the law of assault and battery? Are there any who exercise the virtues of patience and forgiveness, if they can have legal means of punishing the aggressor, and revenging themselves tenfold on the person who gives them the most slight offence? Innumerable are the instances that could be given to show, that the doctrine of the Gospel has very little influence upon the practice of its *followers*; unless it be on a few obscure people, that *nobody knows*. The foregoing formidable objection, therefore, we hope, is pretty well got over, except with the *obscure few* above-mentioned.

But as I would willingly remove every the least shadow of an objection that I am acquainted with, I must take notice of one which was made by a person very zealous indeed for our cause; but who feared, he said, that people would not bear publicly to avow their love of Tormenting, and their disregard of that very religion which they profess. This, at first, almost staggered me, and I was going to throw by my work, till I recollected several books (some too written by divines*) that had been extremely well-received, although they struck at the very foundation of our religion. These precedents are surely sufficient to make me depend upon coming off with impunity, let me publish what I will, except a libel against any great man. For to abuse Christ himself is not, at present, esteemed so high an offence, as to abuse one of his followers; or, rather, one of his *Abusers*; for such may we term all those, who, without observing his laws, call themselves after his name.

It has been already observed, that the torments of the body are not much allowed in civilized nations: but yet, under the notion of punishments for faults, such as whipping and picketing* amongst the soldiers; with some sorts of curious marine discipline, as the cat-of-nine-tails, keelhauling,* and the like; a man may pick out some excellent fun; for if he will now and then inflict those punishments on the good, which were intended for the chastisement and amendment of the bad, he will not only work the flesh, but vex the spirit, of an ingenious youth; as nothing can be more grating to a liberal mind, than to be so unworthily treated.

If I should be so happy, my good pupils, by these my hearty endeavours, as to instruct you thoroughly in the ingenious art of plaguing and tormenting the mind, you will have also more power over the body than you are at first aware of. You may take the Jew's forfeit of a pound of flesh,* without incurring the imputation of barbarity which was cast on him for that diverting joke. He was a mere mongrel at Tormenting, to think of cutting it off with a knife; no—your true delicate way is to waste it off by degrees.—For has not every creditor (by the pleasant assistance of a prison) the legal power of taking ten or twenty pounds of Christian flesh, in forfeit of his bond?

However, without such violent measures, you may have frequent opportunities (by teasing and tormenting) of getting out of your friends a good pretty picking.* But be very careful daily to

---

[1] See *The Merchant of Venice*, written by Shakespeare.*

observe, whether your patient continues in good health, and is fat and well-liken:* if so, you may be almost certain, that your whole labour is thrown away. As soon, therefore, as you perceive this to be the case, you must (to speak in the phrase of surgeons, when they hack and hew a human body) immediately choose another *Subject*.

PART THE FIRST

HE following instructions are divided into two parts. This first part is addressed to those, who may be said to have an exterior power from visible authority, such as is vested, by law or custom, in masters over their servants; parents over their children; husbands over their wives; and many others. The second part will be addressed to those, who have an interior power, arising from the affection of the person on whom they are to work; as in the case of the wife, the friend, &c.

It would be tiresome, and almost endless, to enumerate every connection under the two foregoing heads:* I have therefore taken only a few of the principal ones in each division; and shall begin with masters and mistresses, as in the following chapter.

CHAPTER I

Instructions to Masters and Mistresses, concerning their Servants

As the intercourse between a master and his man is not so frequent as between a lady and her maid, I shall not direct myself to the former, but only give rules to the latter; and where those rules are practicable for the master, I hope he will be so kind as to convert them to his own use.

To scold at and torment *all* your servants appears, at first sight, to be the desirable thing; but those who study the best method of this amusing art, will tell you, that it is much better to select out one or two, at the most, who are proper objects, and who you are sure can feel your strokes; for by this means you may make use of all your bad servants, as instruments to plague the good.

Be sure on no account to make use of any distinction, or ever examine into the true author of any fault or carelessness, unless it be done privately, in order to lay the blame on a wrong person; as for instance;

If you blame Susan the housemaid for having done such a thing, and she should say, 'Indeed, madam, it was not I, but Martha the cook, that did it;' you must raise your voice, and tell her,* 'that you cannot trouble your head to distinguish amongst such low wretches—that *all* servants are careless alike; and if you have any more such accidents in your family,* they shall *all* go.'

If, on blaming any servant for a fault, she should be able to excuse herself, in a manner that ought to be perfectly satisfactory to a reasonable person, you have nothing for it, but to say, 'that you will not hear the impertinent discourse of such a wench— that if she cannot hold her tongue, she is no servant for you—and that you never knew a servant guilty of a fault, but she had pertness and invention enough to make a good excuse for it'*—

then lament, that you do not live in a country, where you might be so happy as to be served by mutes.

Take great care* never to lay the saddle upon the right horse, as this is the most sure and infallible method of galling.

The old saying,

> *Twice I did well, and that I heard never;*
> *Once I did ill, and that I heard ever;*

must by no means be contradicted by *you*; for the oftener you give your servants an opportunity to apply it to themselves, the oftener do you make them feel your power.

The two foregoing rules are of general use likewise to all your friends and acquaintance.

When your servants are sick, you may in earnest be very kind and good to them, as it will greatly contribute towards gaining you the reputation of good nature, and as it is necessary for your own convenience to restore them to health, in order to make them useful. Besides, you may use them ten times the worse for it when they are well, and perpetually upbraid them with your kindness to them when they were ill. As servants, by their way of life, are generally pretty healthy, you need not fear that this practice will go very deep towards exhausting your stock of kindness; for you must take care to have a watchful eye, not to be imposed on by sham sickness; and if a servant falls into a lingering disorder, you have nothing to do but directly to turn them away.

When you hire a footman, be sure to insist upon it, that he pays so strict a regard to your orders, and your *way* in doing everything, that the least deviation in any point should be a forfeit of his place.

This gives frequent opportunities for rating* and scolding; for it is but to make your orders impracticable, and then, be sure not to hear one word he can say in his defence, for not having performed impossibilities. Or you may lay several traps, to tempt him not to adhere strictly to your commands, and then make it a matter of offence, whether he does, or does not.

But this ingenious method of laying traps wants, I believe, farther explanation; let me therefore give you an instance.*

If you go to visit a friend, in a showery day, when the weather is quite uncertain, you may order your footman to come for you at such an hour, and bid him come *without* the coach, for you would walk home. If the weather should prove fair, you must for that day lose your diversion: but if it rains, then your sport begins. Should your footman (thinking it impossible for you to choose walking in the wet and dirt), contrary to your orders, bring you the coach, you may rate him extremely for not observing your orders. You may tell him, that you did not want his care for your health, nor his wisdom to comment on your directions—that all you wanted in a servant was obedience—that you would not for a hundred guineas, have had your horses brought out in such a wet evening. If you are in London, you may say you intended to take a chair;* but if you are in the country, you must declare, that you would rather have walked home two miles through the rain, than have had your poor horses so cruelly exposed: but it was your misfortune to have such wise people about you, that they did not think you knew how to give your own orders.

On the other hand, should the footman, fearful of disobeying your commands, come to you in this wet evening, without the coach; then may you lament your hard fate, in having nothing but fools about you, that could not distinguish in common occurrences.

If you can once catch a servant in this, or any suchlike trap, it gives continual new opportunities of scolding. For if the fault was the adherence to your commands, you may always to your orders add—'But pray remember, I am not such a tyrant and a fool, as you supposed me when you made me walk home in the wet.' And if his fault was the departing from the strict letter of your commands; then to your orders you may add—'But pray mind what I say to you, and not go according to your own wisdom, as you did when you gave my horses cold by bringing them out in the rain.'

If you have no children, keep as large a quantity of tame animals as you conveniently can. If you have children, a smaller number will do.

Show the most extravagant fondness you possibly can for all these animals: and let them be of the most troublesome and mischievous sort, such as cats, monkeys, parrots, squirrels, and little snarling lap-dogs.

Their uses for the Tormenting your servants are various.

In the first place, if they are properly encouraged, and never tamed, they will be so liberal of their teeth and claws, that the servants will, in general, be bit and scratched all over. Then, if your servants should dare to offend one of these favourites, there is a noble field for scolding and rating them: and one farther use, and not one of the least, of these animals, is to feed them with all sorts of rarities, and give them (I mean the dogs and cats) what anyone would be glad of, while you feed your servants with the coarsest and cheapest diet that you can get.

If you happen to have a very good cook, you must strictly enquire into her temper; and if you find her a termagant* (as most cooks are, according to Ben Jonson's observation),* you must give up all hopes of plaguing *her*. You must then find your enjoyment in the good dinners she dresses for you, and the use she will be of to oppress the other servants. If she should be ever so good a cook, and should happen to be good-tempered, you must not let her escape you, but must always send her down word, that your dinner was not eatable. It is true indeed, that, by this means, you may make her leave her place, and you may lose a good servant: but you are no true lover of the noble game of Tormenting, if a good dinner, or any other convenience or enjoyment, can give you half the pleasure, as the teasing and mortifying a good industrious servant, who has done her very best to please you.

But to return to my termagant cook.—When you have such an one, then remember you have a jewel. In the first place, make a favourite of her; for be it observed always, that the very worst amongst your servants is to be your greatest favourite.

Hearken to all the stories she has a mind to tell you, of the rest of the servants; and if any complaint is made against her, say you disbelieve it; adding, that you perceive they are all in a plot against poor Martha the cook; and that they have a mind to distress you, by endeavouring to make you part with the *only* good servant you have; besides intending, you suppose, to poison you with some slut* of their own recommending.

Your housemaid you have so little intercourse with, that I hardly know how to direct your proceedings with regard to her. If you love a clean house, keep a good housemaid, when you can get one; but enquire also concerning her temper. If it is very bad, be sure not to part with her, as she will contribute towards plaguing the other servants: but, if she be a very good-natured obliging girl, and ready to assist her fellow servants, you may tease her about the dirtiness of the house, as I directed with regard to the good-natured cook about her dinners, till you have sent her packing; and you may chance, perhaps, to have better luck with the next.

Scolding at all the servants, as before observed, is too common and vulgar a method; nor is it ever used by your true adepts in the art of Tormenting. But some pretty good proficients in the science have made a favourite of their own maid, and made her the insolent instrument of worrying the rest. This is a tolerable good method, but, in my opinion, not the very best. To know that all the lower part of your family are persecuted and plagued by a taunting creature of your own tutoring, is, without doubt, a pleasant reflection; but yields not half the joy as bringing the game nearer home. If you have a husband, or friend, a toad-eater,* or some grown-up children, to exercise your talents on, you may proceed in the above beaten path, as having work enough already on your hands; and you may then be contented to execute your torments on your lower servants, by suffering that proxy, your own woman, to worry them: but if you have none of the before-mentioned subjects, then most excellent sport will be found from teasing and vexing your own maid, which may be done in the following manner:

Let us suppose, that you have just hired Mrs Jenny to be about your own person: suppose her, also, to be a clean, well-looking, good-natured girl. Be very kind to her for about a week, that you may raise her expectations of leading an easy, quiet life; for in a judicious disappointment lies half the art in every connection whatever. When Jenny is satisfied, by your kind behaviour, that you are very well-disposed towards her, begin some familiar discourse with her; and draw her on to a freedom of speech, that, without such encouragement, would never have come into her head: then fly all at once into a violent rage with her; call her saucy, pert, and impudent; upbraid her with being sprung from a dunghill, and blame yourself for conversing with so low a wretch.

Always scold at her, if she is the least undressed or dirty; and say you cannot bear such beasts about you.

If she is clean and well-dressed, tell her that you suppose she dresses out for the fellows; for the wenches of this age are so forward, that the men can hardly be quiet for them.

Order her to call you in a morning, and, although she comes in ever so softly, fall into a violent passion, because she made such a noise, as to start you suddenly out of your sleep.

If she ever does anything extremely well to please you; as wash your finest lace, or make up your cap, &c. you may commend her very highly for it,—once, but no more.—For you must on no account ever afterward fail to find fault with her, although it be done ever so well. And always, to your finding fault, add a reproach, how well it was done such a time; and how much you then commended her for it; but commendations and praises ever spoil the best servant in the world; it was owing, you may say, to the baseness and ingratitude of servants, that you was forced to put a restraint upon your own natural temper, which prompted you to all sorts of kindness and indulgences: yet your hard case was such, that you could not so much as commend a wench for ironing a cap, but she presently grew careless, and good for nothing, upon it.

Remember always to tease and soothe her so alternately, that she shall be vastly puzzled, whether to be pleased or displeased with her place: but, whenever you have been pretty free with your torments, you must talk of leaving off some old gown, or of some great person's coming to your house; or in some other manner endeavour to awaken her interest, so that she may not leave you.

When you are in high good humour and familiarity with her, you may say, 'That you are not one of those mistresses who never think of diverting their poor servants; and that you intend, therefore, the next day, to take her abroad with you: if in London, to see sights, &c. or if in the country, to walk, or go upon the water with you; or any other way that may come into your head.' Your condescension in making her your companion, will greatly elate her spirits; and your kindness will fill her heart with grateful pleasure. You cannot rob her of the joy she will have in the expectation of this promised favour; but the higher that is raised, the greater will be her disappointment, when the next morning, you contrive to keep her so fully employed, till the moment you are setting out, that it will be impossible for her to get herself ready: then fly into the highest rage imaginable with her, for making you wait; but by no means leave her behind; for that stroke she will soon recover by amusing herself with her fellow servants, and being rid of your scolding; take her therefore with you; and lecture her all the way, on her baseness and ingratitude, in plaguing you in such a manner, in return for your intended kindness. Don't suffer her,* the whole day, to look up, or say her very soul is her own: so that in the midst of this pleasant exped-ition, taken, as you may tell her, by you, out of pure good nature, to please a dirty wench, she may wish to her soul, that she was at home, either in the wash-house, or the scullery, performing the most laborious offices in the lowest station in the family.

But let us suppose the patience of your miserable object quite exhausted, and that she is worked into a proper indifference about pleasing you; so that you should find that she minded very little what you said to her; only (considering yours as a profitable place) that she was resolved to bear all your tricks, for the sake of your money; then part with her directly, and get another: for all the pleasure of Tormenting is lost, as soon as your subject is become insensible to your strokes.

CHAPTER II

To the Patronesses of an Humble Companion

I HAVE often wondered, considering the great number of families there are, whose fortunes are so large, that the addition of one, or even two, would hardly be felt, that they should not more frequently take into their houses, and under their protection, young women who have been well-educated; and who, by the misfortune or death of their friends, have been left destitute of all means of subsistence. There are many methods for young men, in the like circumstances, to acquire a genteel maintenance; but for a girl, I know not of one way of support, that does not, by the custom of the world, throw her below the rank of a gentlewoman.

There are two motives for taking such young women under protection.

One is, the pleasure which ('tis said) kind and benevolent hearts must take in relieving from distress one of their fellow creatures; and, for their repeated kindness and indulgence to an unfortunate deserving person,* receiving the daily tribute of grateful assiduity, and cheerful looks. For I have been informed, by a friend* well-versed in human nature, that, however loud the outcry is against ingratitude for real kindness, yet that true and real kindness seldom or never did excite ingratitude: and moreover, that when those violent outcries came to be examined into, the obliged person had, in fact, been guilty of no ingratitude, or the patron had bestowed no real kindness. Nay, farther, that, should it be proved, that ungrateful returns are sometimes made for real favours, it would commonly be found, upon inquiry, that the persons conferring such favours had a blind side open to flattery, or some other passion; by which means they had shut their eyes, and plucked a poisonous weed to place in their bosoms, instead of using their power of sight and distinction, in order to gather one of those many grateful flowers, which nature has scattered over the face of the earth: the intoxicating quality of which weed has still kept their eyes closed, till they are roused by some racking pain, which it instils into the inmost recesses of the heart.

But, notwithstanding the before-mentioned outcry against ingratitude, there are some, I must confess, who, from compassion and generosity, have taken the distressed into their protection, and have treated them with the highest kindness and indulgence. Nay, I have known a set of tasteless, silly people, who are so void of any relish for this our pleasant game, that they would never wish to see a face in sorrow or tears, unless 'twas in their power to dry those tears, and turn that sorrow into cheerful smiles. But to such insipid folks I write not; as I know my rules, to them, would be of little service. I address myself, therefore, in this chapter, only to those who take young women into their houses, as new subjects of their power.

From the dejection that is so often seen in the countenances of those that live dependent; from Cowley's exclamation against that state, as being the thing that he would wish to his most bitter enemy;* from the anxiety that people show, to possess fortune enough to render themselves independent; may we not infer, that there are many patronesses, who have a true relish for this sport, and who will thank me for these my rules? For although this little book may not help them to one new and untried method of Tormenting; yet it may keep the old ones ready in their minds, to be exerted on all proper occasions.

There is some difficulty in giving rules for tormenting a dependant, that shall differ from those already laid down for plaguing and teasing your servants, as the two stations differ so very little in themselves. The servant, indeed, differs in this; she receives wages, and the humble companion receives none: the servant is most part of the day out of your sight; the humble companion is always ready at hand to receive every cross word that rises in your mind: the servants can be teased only by yourself, your dogs, your cats, your parrots, your children; the humble companion (besides being the sport of all these) must, if

you manage rightly, bear the insults of all your servants themselves; who, the worse you use them, will the more readily use the
power you give them, of revenging themselves on poor Miss
Lucy—

In the first place, let me advise you to be very careful in the
choice of an humble companion; for be it always remembered,
that, in every connection where this art of Teasing and Tormenting is exercised, much depends upon the subject of your
power.

In a servant, you have little to look for but diligence and good
nature; but in a dependant there are many more requisites.

Let her be well-born, and well-educated. The more acquire-
ments she has, the greater field will you have for insolence, and
the pleasure of mortifying her. Out of the numberless families in
the church and army, that outlive themselves, and come to decay,*
great will be your choice. Pick out, if possible, one that has lived a
happy life, under tender and indulgent parents. Beauty, or
deformity; good sense, or the want of it; may any of them, with
proper management, so well answer your purpose, that you need
not be very curious as to that matter: but on no account take into
your house one that has not a tender heart, with a meek and
gentle disposition; for if she has spirit enough to despise your
insults, and has not tender affections enough to be soothed and
melted by your kindness (which must be sparingly bestowed), all
your sport is lost; and you might as well shoot your venom at a
marble statue in your garden.

Although I have supposed, that beauty or deformity, good
sense or folly, in your dependant, are in some measure indifferent,
yet I would have you, if possible, mix them thus: take good sense,
with plainness or deformity; and beauty, with a very weak
capacity.

If your humble companion be handsome, with no great share
of understanding, observe the following directions, towards Miss
Kitty:

Take care seldom to call her anything but 'Beauty', 'Pretty
Idiot', 'Puppet', 'Baby-face'; with as many more of such sarcasti-
cal epithets as you can invent.

If you can ever provoke her enough to show any resentment in her countenance, looking at her with a mixture of anger and contempt, you may say, 'I *beseech* you child to spare your frowns for those who will fear them; and keep your disdainful looks for the footmen when they make love to you;* which, by your flirting airs, I make no doubt they are encouraged to do.'*

If, by your discourse, you move her tears, you may call her 'Weeping beauty'; and ask her, out of what play, or idle romance, she had learnt that tears were becoming. Then drive her out of the room with these words, 'Begone out of my sight, you blubbering fool—*Handsome indeed!* If I had a dog that looked so frightful, I would hang him.'

Although you may, generally, insult her with her beauty, yet be sure, at times, to say so many mortifying things, as shall make her believe you don't think her in the least handsome. If her complexion is fair, call her 'Whey-face'; if she is really an olive beauty,* you may tell her she is as brown as mahogany: if she is inclinable to pale, tell her she always looks as white as a cloth:* and you may add 'That whatever people may fancy of their own sweet persons, yet, in your opinion, there could be no beauty in a whited wall.' In this case, sometimes, insultingly, the name of 'Lily-face!' will come in. If she has a fine bloom, tell her she looks as red-faced, as if she drank brandy; and you have no notion, you may say, of cook-maid beauty. Thus, by right management, every personal perfection may be turned to her reproach. Fine large eyes may be accused of goggling; small ones may be termed unmeaning,* and insignificant; and so of every feature besides. But if she happens to have fine, white, even teeth, you have no resource, but to tell her, whenever you catch her smiling, that she is mighty fond of grinning, to show her white teeth. Then add, 'Pray remember, child, that you can't show your teeth, without showing your folly.' You may likewise declare, that if you had a girl of your own, who showed such a silly vanity, you would flay her alive.

One thing be sure not to omit, although it is ever so false; which is, to tell her, and in the plainest and grossest terms, that she has (oh shocking accusation to a fine girl!) sweaty feet, and a nauseous breath.*

To a young creature of beauty, and any degree of delicacy, nothing can be more teasing and grating to hear, than this. From the extreme mortification she must feel, 'tis ten to one but she will deny it, with some resentment, or will shed tears of vexation for the charge: these will both equally serve your purpose. If the first, you have many ways to deal with her. Furious scolding and abuse is no bad method, if not too lately practised; but insulting taunts, I think, will do rather better. Such as follow:

'Oh to be sure! you are too delicate a creature to have any human failings? you are all sweetness and perfection! well, heaven defend me from such *sweet* creatures!' Then changing your tone and looks into fierceness, you may proceed; 'I tell you, Madam Impertinence, whatever you may think, and how impudently soever you may dare to contradict me in this manner, that all your nasty odious imperfections have been often taken notice of by many people besides myself, though nobody had regard enough for you, to tell you of such things.—You may toss your head, and look with as much indignation as you please; but these airs, child, will not do long with me.—If you don't like to be told of your faults, you must find some other person to support you. So pray, for the present, walk off to your own apartment; and consider whether you choose to lay aside that pretty, becoming resentment of yours; or to be thrown friendless, as I found you, on the wide world again.—You must not be told of your failings, truly, must

---

[1] To those who are displeased at the indelicacy of the above expression, with some others that follow, and would wish them omitted, I can only say, in the words of Butler a little altered,

> *And though some critic here cries shame,*
> *And says our author is to blame,*
>
> Hudibras, I. ii. 379–80
>
> *To such I answer, cruel fate*
> *Tells me thy counsel comes too late.**
>
> I. iii. 585–6.

Or, in plain prose, 'tis desired to be remembered, that 'tis the lady patroness, and not our author, that uses such coarse language.

you! Oh I would not have such a proud heart as thine is in my breast, for the world! Though let me tell you, Mistress Minx,* 'twould much better become my station, than yours.'

For fear this kind and gentle speech of yours should have wounded too deeply; and Miss Kitty should really, on consideration, prefer wandering, beggary, or the most menial service, to such a life of dependence, and you should thereby lose your game, be sure not to let it be above half an hour before you send your woman upstairs to her, with some sweetmeats, fruit, or anything you know she is fond of. Order your woman, if she finds her in a rage, to soften her mind, till she brings her to tears; then to comfort her; and tell her how kindly you had been just then talking of her; and to leave no means untried to coax her down. You must then receive her with the highest good humour; and tell her, you intend for her some new clothes, a pleasant jaunt, or any indulgence, that you know would please her: continue this good humour so strongly, that she shall not have the least opportunity of telling you, what, undoubtedly, she must have resolved above-stairs; namely, that she could live with you no longer. And if this fit of kindness be carried into a proper excess, the poor girl will, at last, begin to think herself to blame; and that you are the kindest, best creature to her in the world. Then is she properly prepared for the next Torment you shall think fit to inflict.

Should Miss Kitty, on the mortifying accusation before-mentioned, burst into tears, you must proceed in a contrary method: and, in a soft and gentle accent, you may say to her, 'I cannot imagine, my dear, what should make you cry, when I am only kindly telling you, as a friend, of some misfortunes you cannot possibly help. I am very far from blaming you, my love; for although, I thank heaven, I am myself free from all such shocking and disagreeable things, yet nobody pities people with such imperfections more than I do.'* You might here, also, aggravate the misfortune it was, to so young and so pretty a girl, to have such personal defects: for (you may add) that you had often heard the men declare (and you thought 'em very much in the right), that they should prefer the ugliest girl that ever was born, who was sweet in her person, to the greatest beauty upon earth, with such nauseous, disgustful imperfections.

If Miss Kitty, in the midst of her sobs, should find her voice enough to deny the charge, you may go on as follows:

'I don't wonder, my dear, that you are not sensible of these things yourself; 'tis a very common case: but you should, therefore, take it more kind of those who will tell you of them.—Come, don't cry, my dear child, about it any more: hearken to me; and I'll try to comfort you, if I can. You know, my love, I have often told you how dreadful a situation a girl of your beauty would be in, should you lose my protection: how many would be the snares then laid for your ruin! How likely is it, that, in time, you would be deserted by those base wretches your seducers! You know I have often wept, from my dreadful apprehensions for you, lest you should come to walk London streets.*—But dry up your eyes; I have better hopes for you, Miss Kitty; for these ugly things I have been telling you of (and which, I assure you, are greatly taken notice of already) will, when they once come to be known, secure you more against the addresses of that destroyer man, than even extreme old age and ugliness.'

With this jargon* of insult, reproach, and seeming tenderness, the girl's heart will be ready to burst; nor will she be able to form any kind of reply. You may then continue the same farce; take her by the hand; say you are sorry you had even mentioned such things to her, as your discourse seemed so much to affect her: bid her take care to change her stockings very often, and not come too near you with her breath; and you would promise her, that you never would speak to her about either any more.

This promise remember strictly to keep: but yet you may take frequent opportunities of mortifying her, even in a room full of company; by vehemently inveighing against those very things of which you had accused her. You may go so far as to say, that you know an exceeding pretty girl, who has all those misfortunes; but you love her so well, you would not, for the world, expose her by naming her name; yet, by kind nods upon Miss Kitty, the whole room will understand your meaning. You may also, whenever she comes near you, hastily take snuff, or smell to your sans-pareil;*

then look at her, rather with pity than any kind of anger; and, by this means, you may keep her in such a continual mortified state, that you will very seldom need any other strokes of your power: unless indeed she happens to receive any particular address from the young gentlemen who visit at your house, with due commendations of her person, and genteel appearance: which will, in all probability, so elate her mortified spirits, that you must have another trial of skill with her, to fetch her down.

So far for a handsome girl. But,

If plainness, with a good share of natural parts, should be the lot of this your dependant, whom we will call Miss Fanny, great scope will you have, in a different way, for Tormenting, Teasing, and Plaguing her.

You must begin with all sorts of mortifying observations* on her person; and frequently declare, that you hate anything about you that is not agreeable to look at. This, in the beginning, will vex the girl; first, as 'tis not very pleasant to have a mirror perpetually held to our view, where the reflection is so mortifying: and next, as she will really be sorry to find herself disagreeable to a person she would wish to please. But in time she will find you out: she will perceive the malice of such reflections; and, if she has good sense, will get above any concern about what you can say of her person. As soon as you perceive this, change your method; and level most of your darts against her understanding. Never let a day pass, without calling her, in that day, a *Wit*, at least a hundred times. Begin most requests, or rather commands, with these sort of phrases, 'Will your *Wisdom* please to do so or so, &c. Can a lady of your *fine parts* condescend to darn this apron? Would it not be too great a condescension for a *Wit*, to submit to look over my housekeeper's accounts?' Whatever answer she makes to these things; whether it be showing a little resentment for such insolent treatment; or saying, with mildness, that she is ready to do anything you command her; let your reply be—'I don't hear, child, what you say.—However, I presume it was something mighty smart and witty.—But let me give you one piece of advice; which is, to be more sparing of your tongue, and less sparing of your labour, if you expect a continuance of my favour to you—'

Although your chief mark* is her understanding; yet I would not have you quite drop your reflections on the plainness of her person: for, by continual teasing, you may possibly bring her to say something to the following effect:—That she could not help the plainness of her person:—That she endeavoured to be as contented as she could; but, in short, she did not much concern herself about the matter.—Then have you a double road for Teasing her still more on that head.

If she is clean and well-dressed, you may put on a malicious sneer; and, looking her over from top to toe, you may noddle* your head; and say, 'So, Miss, considering you are a *Wit*, and a lady who despises all personal advantages, I must needs say you have tricked* yourself out pretty handsomely today.' Then may you add, that you would hold a good wager, she was every day longer prinking* in the glass than you was.—But it was always so.—You had ever observed, that the ugliest women were much fonder of their persons, than the most beautiful.

If she fails in the least particular of nicety in dress, then have you the old beaten path before you: load her with the names of trollop, slattern, slut, dirty beast, &c. Omit not any of those trite observations; that all *Wits* are slatterns;—that no girl ever delighted in reading, that was not a slut;—that well might the men say they would not for the world marry a *Wit*; that they had rather have a woman who could make a pudden,* than one who could make a poem;—and that it was the ruin of all girls who had not independent fortunes, to have learnt either to read or write. You may tell her also, that she may thank God, that her ugliness will preserve her from being a whore.—Then conclude all these pious reflections with thanking heaven, that, for your part, you are no *Wit*; and that you will take care your children shall not be of that stamp.

To a girl of this sort your fits of kindness must be much more frequent than to any other: for if she has sense, 'tis ten to one, but she will have spirit enough to throw off her chains, if they always appear made of iron: you must therefore gild them over with great real indulgences; and never let your ill usage rest long enough upon her mind, to bring her to a proper resolution. Show also great tenderness and affection to her before company; that if ever she should leave you, she may be generally accused of the highest ingratitude.

I know not whether it would not be best, if the girl has so much spirit, that you are forced to bestow a vast deal of kindness on her, to urge her temper far enough to make her run away. For although it is noble sport to have a girl of sense to work upon, yet 'tis warm exercise;* and, by turning such a one adrift, and taking another of less understanding into your service, you will have a fine opportunity, in all companies, of not only raving at the ingratitude of Miss Fanny, who is gone, but of extolling your own extreme good nature, in taking Miss Dolly, who is now with you. Besides, you will have some new, pleasant, additional taunts, for Miss Dolly: as thus,—If ever you should scold at her, and tease her enough to make her say the least word in answer, you may say, 'Heigh-day! What!—you too are going to be a girl of spirit, are you? I shall hear, I suppose, that you have taken your flight, after the witty Miss Fanny.—But pray troop off as soon as you please, Madam.—I shall not send for you back.—But I hope I shall, in time, be convinced of my own folly, in thinking there is such a thing as gratitude in this world.'

Should your humble companion be a plain girl, with a very moderate degree of understanding, and great meekness of temper, you have little to do but to rate and mortify her continually; only tempering your ill humour with just kindness enough to keep her your own. Much less of that ingredient called kindness will do in this, than in the two other cases: for, being sensible of her own defects, such a girl will most likely pine away her very soul, and lose all her spirit in grieving at your ill usage, without thinking herself capable of any redress by leaving you. As soon as she is become a poor dejected wretch, that trembles at every word you say to her, a little Teasing every day will do; and the words Dolt, and Mope,* properly applied, will be sufficient. But remember to keep her as much in your sight as possible; because the only chance of comfort she can have, is in being out of your presence.

The foregoing directions are adapted to particular quali-fications in your dependant: but I will now add a few general rules, that will be suitable to any girl who is under your command.

Carefully watch in what things your humble companion is most diligent to please you; and be sure never to appear pleased with any such endeavours.

There are some girls so very observant of your commands, and so ready cheerfully to do everything you desire them, that 'tis very difficult to catch them at a fault. If you should observe this disposition in Miss Lucy, you may practise a game which many people who honour themselves with the name of humourists, have played before you: this is, never to tell anyone what you want; but to be extremely angry, that your servants, your dependants and friends, have not the gift of divination.

Surround yourself with as many peculiarities as you possibly can; and this not with a design of being pleased (as some odd people are) with those dependants, who, observing all such your peculiarities, hope by that means to please you: but in order to have more frequent opportunities of rating your servants, or teasing your humble companion, as in the following manner.

Declare, whether true or false, that you have a great hatred to a noise; and whenever Miss Lucy steps more softly than common, in order to please you, tell her you wonder how she can stamp about the floor in such a manner, as if she had wooden shoes on. Or, if you choose not to imagine that she stepped loud, then you may scream out, as soon as she comes near you, and say, that she has frightened you out of your wits; for she glided in so softly, that you took her for a ghost. If also you observe, that she is uniformly careful never to offend your ears, by any noise that she can possibly avoid, you must never omit saying to her, whenever she goes out of the room, 'Let me *entreat* you, child, not to bounce the door* after you, enough to shake the house.' But you may suffer your own children to make as much noise as they please, without any kind of reproof.

If the children, or the servants, make any complaints against Miss Lucy, be sure not to hear one word she attempts to say, in her own defence.

If the complaint comes from your servants, tell her that you wonder at her assurance, in speaking to any of your servants: Or with a sneer, ask her if she supposes that you keep servants to wait upon her.

If the complaint against her comes from the children, scold her (as we say) within an inch of her life. Ask her, how she dares to affront your children? Abuse her, even in the language of Billingsgate,* calling her all the scurrilous names you can invent; such as draggle-tail low-bred creature, scum of the earth, with as many more abusive terms as you can recollect. Then drive her with great impetuosity out of your sight.

These violent passions of scolding I would by no means advise to be too often repeated in this case, any more than to your servants, as they would soon lose their force, and subject you to contempt. But they do extremely well, to come in now and then, by way of variety and surprise; especially in this connection, as they are more adapted to frighten half out of her wits a good-natured inoffensive girl well-born, and well-bred, than the lower sort of servants: who, if they should chance to have been brought up near Billingsgate or St Giles's,* might have been accustomed to such sort of language.

If your son, Master Jacky, should have cut Miss Lucy across the face with his new knife; or your daughter, Miss Isabella, should have pinched her arms black and blue, or scratched her face and neck, with her pretty nails, so as to have fetched the blood; and poor Lucy, to prevent any farther mischief to her person, should come and make her complaint to you; do you, in the first place, rate her soundly for provoking the poor children, who, you may affirm, are the best-natured little things in the world, if they are not teased and vexed. But if by the blood streaming from her face or arms, it appears plainly that the girl has been very much hurt, you may (to show your great impartiality) say, that you will send for the children in, and reprimand them. 'For it is not my way', you may say, 'to suffer the *lowest* creature in my house to be ill-used; nor will I, on any account permit *my* children to behave themselves unbecoming their station.' Miss Lucy, on this (not comprehending perhaps the full drift of your prologue),* will brighten up a little; will thank you for your indulgence; and, if a good-natured girl, will beg you not to be too severe with master and miss, who, she hopes, on being spoke to, will do so no more. Now let your countenance grow very fierce; ring the bell most furiously; then sternly order the children to be brought before you; and utter such threats, as will make poor Miss Lucy tremble for the consequence, and heartily repent of her complaint.

But how will she be surprised, if you act this scene well!

As soon as the children come into the room, begin to rate them most severely.—But for what?—Why for disobeying your commands, and condescending to play, and be familiar, with anything but their equals! You may conclude also, by threatening them with the greatest punishment, if ever they are again guilty of so high an offence, as that of speaking to a wretch so much beneath them in birth, fortune, and station, as Miss Lucy.

If you have no children, keep dumb animals enough, and they will pretty near answer all your purposes.

It is not amiss, if your dependant be a girl very apt to blush, to be perpetually, before company, saying things to her, that will keep her in a constant confusion of face, which is as teasing and uneasy a sensation as may be.*

Another pleasant way before company is to rail so loudly against laziness, ill temper, or any other bad quality, that, you may say, *all* girls possess, that your visitors will go away, convinced that poor Lucy is the plague and torment of your life.

If you have chosen a girl (as at first advised) whose parents, when living, were truly kind and indulgent to her, you may amuse yourself with a fine game at compassion with her, as follows:

Begin talking to her of her parents; raise all her tender affections; collect every little circumstance that will awaken her grief, and dissolve her into tears, by painting her loss in the liveliest colours. Carry the scene so far, as to mingle tears with hers; and utter the strongest professions, of being to her, yourself, a second father, mother, friend, and protectress. The poor girl's heart will

---

[1] This hint was given me by a female friend, who insisted on my inserting it; although I assured her, that the rule was quite needless, as blushing is full as much out of date as high heads.*

be almost melted with tender sorrow for the loss of her parents, and with overflowing gratitude to you for your goodness. But, as soon as the latter has, by degrees, begun to overspread her mind with a joy, that will in a manner dispel her sorrow; can you, my dear pupil, carry this pleasant sport so high, as in that instant to change your kind behaviour? To grow in a rage with her for nothing; and to make the girl more sensible than before of the loss of indulgent parents, by the cruel reverse she now so strongly experiences? If you can do this, you shall have the highest seat in my temple, and I will say,

>*—Duris genuit te cautibus horrens*
>*Caucasus, Hyrcanæque admôrunt ubera tigres.**

Virgil, *Æneid*, iv. 366–7

CHAPTER III

To Parents

I T has been said, that the state of children when very young, with regard to their parents, is like the state of a blind man, in the hands of a friend who has the use of his eyes. Children want both protection from harms, and direction in every step they are to take. They are perfectly helpless, and incapable of supporting themselves, even one day, without a parental care over them; and where that care is exerted for their benefit, there they undoubtedly owe the highest duty and regard imaginable.

The most unlimited power was ever given to parents over their children: and in ancient Rome, it was said to extend to life and death.* This most probably must arise from a knowledge of the great natural affection and tenderness, that is in almost every living creature towards its offspring; and to such parents as possess this true affection, I direct not my precepts; for where real love and affection towards the children (which must exert itself for their good) is in the heart, all my instructions will be thrown away. But as for you, O ye parents, who are willing to learn, and who intend to make a proper use of your power, let me remind you, that even in this age you are invested, both by law and custom, with the strongest outward and visible power I know of in this land. Purchased slaves are not allowed:* your servants if you use them ill may leave you, or can, in many cases, have better redress against you from the magistrate, than you can procure against them. Your children have nobody to fly to, nobody even to complain to! and as it is in your power to take care of these, or cruelly to neglect them; their very lives, while infants, are still in a manner at your disposal. It is at your own option to feed them on bread and water, the hard fare appointed for criminals, or to pamper them (if you can afford it) with all the dainties of the land. The reins of restraint are yours. The

rod of correction is given into your hands: who shall set bounds
to your strokes?

These my rules—which positively forbid not only all manual
correction, but every the least degree of restraint or contradiction
to the infant's wayward will, if you intend to breed them up
properly, so as to be a torment to themselves if they live, and a
plague to all your acquaintance.

Severity to children, when carried to excess, may, indeed,
render the lives of those children very miserable; and I allow it to
be *one* method of Tormenting; but, in my opinion, by no means
the best.

Yet, if you intend to follow this method, let me give you one
necessary piece of advice: which is, never to strike or whip a child,
but when you are angry, and in a violent passion with that child;
nor ever let this correction come for lying, obstinacy, or disobedi-
ence, in the child, but for having torn or dirtied her white frock, if
it be a girl; or for having accidentally broken a china cup at play;
or any such trifling offence. But there is one strong reason still
remains against the least degree of general severity; which is, the
regard you ought to have for your own reputation. If your intention be to indulge yourself, without any regard to your child's
welfare, why should you take a method by which you may incur
the censure of cruelty, when you can more effectually answer
your own purpose, and be called kind? Therefore, by all means,
humour every child you have to the highest degree, till they attain
the age of five or six years; by which time you will be able to
judge, whether your indulgence has had a proper effect. If you
see them possessed with a due degree of obstinacy, wilfulness,
perverseness, and ill humour; if you find, that the passions of
pride, cruelty, malice, and envy have, like rank weeds, flourished
for want of rooting up, and overwhelmed every spark of goodness
in the mind; then may you (as my true disciples) rejoice in having
so far done your duty by them, as to have laid the proper foundation for their becoming no small adepts in this our useful science.

If, notwithstanding the uncontrolled licence you have given to
your children, of indulging every rising passion, one of them
should chance to be endued with such a mildness of disposition,

and so much in-bred good nature, as to have grown up gentle, against your consent; then, to that child, immediately change your method; grow morose and severe; make favourites of all the rest, and encourage them to tease and insult it, till you have quite broken its spirit, and got the better of its natural placidness of disposition, so as to turn it into a dejected mope.

But take another view of this extreme indulgence to children; and it is hoped this picture will confirm you in such a practice.

Suppose your stock of children too large; and that, by your care for their support, you should be abridged of some of your own luxuries and pleasures. To make away with the troublesome and expensive brats, I allow, would be the desirable thing: but the question is, how to effect this without subjecting yourself to that punishment which the law has thought proper to affix to such sort of jokes. Whipping and starving, with some caution, might do the business: but, since a late execution for a fact of that kind may have given a precedent for the magistrates to examine into such affairs, you may, by these means, find your way to the gallows, if you are low enough* for such a scrutiny into your conduct: and, if you are too high to have your actions punished, you may possibly be a little ill spoken of amongst your acquaintance. I think, therefore, it is best not to venture either your neck or your reputation, by such a proceeding; especially as you may effect the thing, full as well, by following the directions I have given, of holding no restraint over them.

Suffer them to climb, without contradiction, to heights from whence they may break their necks: let them eat everything they like, and at all times; not refusing them the richest meats, and highest* sauces, with as great a variety as possible; because even excess in one dish of plain meat cannot, as I have been told by physicians, do much harm. Suffer them to sit up as late as they please at night, and make hearty meat-suppers; and even in the middle of the night, if they call for it, don't refuse the poor things some victuals. By this means, nobody can say you starve your children: and if they should chance to die of a surfeit, or of an ill habit of body, contracted from such diet, so far will you be from censure, that your name will be recorded for a kind and indulgent parent. If any impertinent person should hint to you, that this manner of feeding your children was the high road to their destruction, you may answer, 'That the poor people suffer their children to eat and drink what they please, not feeding them upon bread-pudden, milk and water, and such stuff, as the physicians advise; and', you may say, 'where do you see anything more healthful, than the children of the poor?' Take my word for it, you may make this appeal without fear of contradiction; for often have I heard it made in company, and never yet did I hear it observed, that the poor, in truth, had not the hurtful things to give their children, which it is in the power of the rich to indulge them in; that the food of these healthy poor children generally is bread and cheese, plain bread, a little fat bacon, clear water, or some small-beer,* hardly removed one degree from water itself; and not roast meat, fish, hashes,* soups, &c. &c. But to return to my farther directions.

On no account miss that useful season of the year the summer; in which you may give your children as much fruit as they can cram down their throats: then be sure not to contradict the poor little things, if they should choose to play about, and overheat themselves, in the middle of the day; and afterwards should choose to cool their limbs, by sprawling about on the wet grass, after the dew is fallen. If they should chance, after all this, to outlive the month of September, without the worms, a fever, the smallpox, or a general corruption of blood, that no medicine can purify, you must wait the event of another summer. From having indulged them in all their humours, you have one chance more of losing them in sickness than those parents have, who control them; which is, that it is not (you know) in the power of medicine to cure, when it is not in your power to get that medicine down the child's throat. On all considerations, therefore, I believe, we may venture to affirm, that letting children entirely alone to their own wills, without the least degree of restraint or contradiction, is the surest road to lead them to their own destruction.

If parents, in the foregoing process, should be able, with truth, to deny the motive I have assigned, can they, with equal truth, deny the probable consequence, here shown, of such indulgence?

Supposing your child, or children, to outlive all these your kind indulgences, encourage them in all sorts of cruelty; first to flies and birds, then to dogs, cats, or any other animals, that come in their way. This will habituate them to that true hardness of heart, which is the foundation of our science.

So pleasant is the sport of Tormenting domestic animals under our protection, that a whole chapter of instructions for that purpose should have been inserted, had it not been already very well exemplified in *Pompey the Little*.* And if my readers have the gift of imitation, they may, by many pleasant examples, become perfect in this practice.

Although I would have you inculcate early into your children's breasts the love of cruelty,* yet, by no means, call it by its true name; but encourage them in the practice of it under the name of *Fun*. When they are well-versed in this sport of Tormenting amongst animals, they may introduce it, under the aforesaid name, amongst their friends and acquaintance. It will equally answer in all stations; for how many hurt shins, bloody noses, broken heads, if not broken bones, has this sport caused at a country wake?* and, in politer life, how many heavy hearts have retired from company, by the means of joke, repartee, and *Fun*?

And that this kind of *Fun* is allowed to be extremely diverting, appears from its being so very common to hear people publicly declare, that they always laugh at mischief.

If your children happen to have but weak understandings, upbraid them with every excellence you see abroad; and lament your own hard fate in being plagued with idiots. But,

If you see a rising genius in any child (especially if it be a girl), unless you can in some way turn it to your own profit, give that child no assistance nor encouragement; but browbeat all endeavours towards striking out of the common road.

When once your children are grown up to men or women's estate,* let the very appearance of indulgence vanish; and, as soon as they are come to a relish of this world's enjoyment, restrain them with a heavy hand. Upbraid them, also, with your former

¹ Bk. I, ch. 9.*

kindness; lament that your past indulgence to them, when children, has made them ungrateful; and declare them to be the grief and torment of your old age.

As you never contradicted or rebuked them, when children, remember that you have in store a large quantity of contradiction and rebukes at their service; of both which be as lavish as possible, particularly of the latter, which will now be of no sort of service; especially if you bestow such rebukes on them before company, and in the roughest terms.

Study the tempers of your sons and daughters, to see what they most delight in; and, as you have an absolute restraining power, exercise it where it will be most strongly felt.

If gaiety and public diversion are their delight, confine them constantly at home; or let them out with such restrictions as will damp all their joy. But if they have no immoderate love for such amusement, and could be as well-contented at home, from the satisfaction they would take in doing their duty, let your chief point be to dress them out, and send them abroad, for your own honour and credit; and receive them with ill humour when they come home. If their chief joy be in endeavouring, by their cheerful conversation, to please and amuse you, put on such a rigid austerity, as shall make them afraid to open their lips before you; and withhold from them the least appearance of pleasure or good humour in yourself, for their readiness in all things to comply with your will.

Spare no expense in dress and equipage for them, provided their dispositions are such, that it will give them no pleasure: for how must an old Harlowe enjoy himself in loading a Clarissa with money, clothes, jewels, &c. whilst he knows, that all she wants from him, is kind looks, and kind words!*

When your daughter comes to be old enough to marry, if she should happen to have fixed her affections on a real deserving young man, and you should be bent upon her giving her hand to one whose only merit is his riches, the behaviour of old Western to his daughter Sophia, in *Tom Jones*, will show you how a fond father should treat a deserving child.*

There is more difficulty in giving positive rules for the

Tormenting children,* than any other connection whatever; as my pupils must have two points to carry: one is, the child's own discomfort; and the other is, the use they are of in Tormenting all your friends and acquaintance. Should you follow the road of those parents, who hold a proper restraint, and keep a watchful eye, over their children, in order to prevent their hurting themselves; should you make that parent your example, who, by carefully watching every rising passion, accustoms the child (if not to subdue) at least to keep it within proper bounds; should you act in the manner of those parents, who, by cultivating and encouraging every good disposition in their children, breed them up with modesty and gentleness of mind; and who, by well-placed kindness and *real* indulgence, have inspired them with a grateful and affectionate regard towards themselves; children thus educated would, I confess, when grown up, in all probability, be more fitted to receive your Torments, than those bred up by my rules. But many contingencies might then arise to prevent the exercise of your power: as your own death, your son's going out in the world, or your daughter's marriage. I give it once more, therefore, as my advice, that you should leave such kind of education for those who have no relish for our sport; and that you pursue the method called *indulgence*, which I have already marked out. This will infallibly make them miserable while infants; as common experience must show you, that no children are so fretful, peevish, and uneasy, as those who are so indulged. And although you may, by this means, breed up a parcel of headstrong, hard-hearted cubs, who, when old enough, will defy your power; yet you may, in the meantime, amuse yourself with your servants, your acquaintance, and your friends, who may chance to be more fitted by nature, or education, for your purpose. You may go out of the world, also, with the pleasing reflection, that you have left behind you a set of wolves, cats, and foxes, of your own educating; who will help to plague and torment all the rest of mankind.

The reason there is no chapter of instructions to children, how to plague their parents, we presume, is pretty obvious. First, because, when they are very young, they cannot read. It lies, therefore, upon you, O ye parents! to make them, in their infancy, both a plague to themselves, and all around them. In the next place, when they are grown old enough to profit by my instructions, they may find, in some of the succeeding chapters, most of the rules that could possibly be given them: which, it is hoped, they will be so kind as to practise on all those parents, who, by departing from my institutes, have given their children an affectionate power over them: for such power will the children gain, if you turn your parental authority into an affectionate friendship towards them.

Could I be so happy as to prevail with you to follow my directions, no other instructions would hereafter be necessary. For ye must be sensible, O ye parents! how much it is in your power to form the minds of your children so as to enrol them under my list, or to guard their tender minds against my precepts, if Solomon was in the right when he said, *Train up your child*, &c.*

CHAPTER IV

To the Husband

THE visible power of the husband comes next to that of the parent: for I think it has been determined in our public courts of justice, by some unpolite professors of the law, that a husband may exercise his marital authority so far, as to give his wife moderate correction.

How happy is it for English wives, that the force of custom is so much stronger than our laws! How fortunate for them, that the men, either through affection, or indolence, have given up their legal rights; and have, by custom, placed all the power in the wife!

Mistake me not so much, as to think that I intend to assert there are no tyrannical or bad husbands; daily experience would soon contradict such an assertion. But the sport of Tormenting is not the husband's chief game. If he grows indifferent to his wife, or comes to hate her, he wishes her dead, or absent; and therefore, if in low life, often takes such violent measures, as to break her bones, or to break her heart: and if in high life; he keeps mistresses abroad, and troubles not his head, one way or other, about his wife.

But there are a set of men in a middle station, who cannot, on account of their fortunes, or reputation, well follow either of the above-mentioned methods: and to such (if there are any amongst them who are not governed* by their wives) I address this chapter; and hope to hit off a few strokes that may be fit for their practice.

It has been already endeavoured to be shown, in what manner a patroness may plague an humble companion; but in the married state, it has, sometimes, been the practice of the husband, to take into his house (I will not say into his bed) a female *humble* companion to torment his wife. If he chooses this method of proceeding, let him select a handsome vixen; and there are, I believe, few female spirits who will accept of such an office, but, without the help of my precepts, will thoroughly answer the husband's purpose in that situation, of plaguing, vexing, and insulting his wife as much as he can possibly desire.

My rules (as before observed) will in this connection be of little use in high life, as it is seldom the concern amongst the great (with some few exceptions) either to please or plague each other: but, in a more moderate degree, husbands may proceed in the following manner.

The best foundation to work on, is to be sure to mistake your wife's character, praise her for what she does not deserve, and overlook every good quality she is in reality possessed of. As it is a very common practice, for women to pretend a dislike to smoking, only because their husbands are fond of it, so do you take care to observe, whether your wife likes or dislikes tobacco: if the smoke of it should really make her sick, which is sometimes the case, be sure never to be without a pipe in your mouth, and rail most heartily at the affectation of *all* wives, who pretend not to love the smell of tobacco. Never let the time of dinner pass, without being displeased with everything that comes to the table. You may blame your wife for the fault of the fishmonger, the poulterer, the butcher, and the cook; particularly the latter, as it gives an ill-natured wench, (who hears from the footman this your kind and tender practice) an opportunity of wreaking her spleen* on her mistress, by the wrong-headed anger of her master.

Give the highest commendations to everything you meet with abroad; and if your wife, thinking to please you, should provide the same things for you at home, be doubly displeased with such things; and declare, that the reason you are so much abroad, and spend so much time in a tavern, is, that by the negligence of your wife you are half-starved at your own table.

If you have a very careful prudent wife, one who by her good economy confines all the expenses under her inspection fairly within her appointment, part with your money to her, like so many drops of your blood; and read her a lecture on extravagance, for every necessary that is bought into the house; at the same time sparing no expense for your own hounds, horses, or claret, to treat your brother sportsmen.

Should you have been abroad for the whole, or any part, of the day, be sure to come home in an exceeding ill humour, if you have a wife at home who knows how to value your good humour. The more cheerfully she receives you, the more sour and morose do you grow upon the same: or, if you choose not to carry the joke so high, a sullen discontent, with several yawns expressive of indifference, will do very well.* Besides, for this latter behaviour, nobody can blame you, as it will (by custom) be set down to the account of low spirits, or some violent fatigue you may have undergone. It has been observed, that more fidelity is often found in the bad part of mankind to the bad, than in the good to the good.* It is also, I believe, as true, that much more tenderness and indulgence is generally exerted towards the counterfeits of any weakness or distress, than to those who labour under a real weakness of body, or affliction of mind. These are facts; let the searchers into human nature declare their causes. But in this wilful want of distinguishing, lies the chief power of tormenting.

If polygamy was allowed, greatly could this chapter be enlarged; for fine sport might a man have among many wives, by confounding their characters, being fond of the bad, being cruel to the good, with several other very pleasant amusements. And that some husbands have a good notion of this kind of diversion, we may, I think justly* infer from what we now see, with regard to those who have had two, three, or four wives in succession. For, if ever you hear, that a man has made an exceeding good husband to one wife, and an exceeding bad husband to another, let the matter be examined into, and it will generally be found, that his indulgence and fondness were placed on an high-spirited vixen, or a wayward insipid doll; whilst his neglect, his ill humour, and his cruelty, were all bestowed on a meek-spirited wife, whose affection and regard for him made her deserve better treatment.

As things are now circumstanced,* my rules for the husband can be but few.

However, should a man happen to have a very deserving woman for his wife, I think I can recommend this our art to him, as productive of some diversion. But as his power would then arise, not so much from his exterior authority, as from the tender affection of his wife;* I must still beg the favour of all those husbands, who intend to study this our science, that they would collect rules for themselves, from any of the chapters that may hit their case, in the second division of this work.

End of Part the First

PART THE SECOND

THIS second part is addressed to those, who have no legal or exterior authority, but who may be said to have an interior power arising from the affection of the person, with whom they are connected. This power, if properly used for the torment of those whose affections you have gained, will be found strong enough greatly to over-balance any exterior power; and is indeed so effectual for the purpose I recommend, that in the case of the husband no one carried this sport very far, but by dropping his marital authority, and teasing his wife through her real love and regard for him.

A few of the connections only are taken in this second division; and we will begin with that of the lover, as in the following chapter.

CHAPTER I

To Lovers

THIS connection gives so large a field for the exercise of our pleasant art, that it cannot be passed over in silence: yet very short will be this chapter; for does anyone want directions in what he is already perfect? Who is there that cannot, without my help, carry his food to his mouth, or perform the office of respiration; Teasing and Tormenting is the sustenance, the breath, the very life, of most young women who are sure of the affections of their lovers. Nor are the men less expert at the practice of Teasing, when they know themselves to be the objects of a woman's love.

Give me leave, therefore, only to pay my compliments to these my best adepts; begging that the ladies, if they find their memory or invention at a loss for a true coquette-behaviour,* would read over most of our comedies since the Restoration;* and that they would not fail to make the favourite characters of such comedies their exemplars.

CHAPTER II

To the Wife

THE common disposition with which a married couple generally come together (except for mere lucrative motives) is this.

The man, for some qualification, either personal or mental, which he sees, or dreams he sees,* in some woman, fixes his affections on that woman: then, instead of endeavouring to fix her affections on himself, he directs all her thoughts, and her enjoyment, on settlements, equipage,* fine clothes, and every other gratification of vanity within his power and fortune to give her. He pays so thorough an adoration and submission to her in all respects, that he soon perfects a work before half-finished* to his hands; namely, the making her completely and immovably in love with—herself.—This puts her, for the present, into such good spirits, and good humour, that the poor man, from the pleasure he finds in her company, believes her to be in love with him. This thought, joined to his first inclination to her person, creates in him a pretty strong affection towards her, and gives her that power over him, which I would willingly assist her in exerting. This affection, when he becomes her husband, generally shows itself in real kindness. But as soon as all the joy arising from courtship is gone, the wife generally grows uneasy; her husband, being no longer her lover, grows disgustful to her; and, if she be a woman of violent passions, she turns fractious and sour; and a breach soon ensues. The husband may bluster, and rave, and talk of his authority and power, as much as he pleases; but it is very easy to grow into such a perfect disregard of such storms, that, by wrapping one's self up in a proper degree of contempt, they will

[1] *Aut videt, aut vidisse putat*—*
Virgil, *Æneid*, vi. 454.

blow as vainly over our heads, as the wind over our houses. Besides, if there are not emoluments enough in the husband's house, to make it worthwhile to bear the ill humours raised by our own frowardness,* separation is the word; to which if a husband will not consent, a cause of cruelty against him, in Doctors Commons,* will soon bring him to; for (as I have heard) the husband there, by paying the expenses of both sides, will be obliged, in a manner, to supply his wife with the means of carrying her own point, and will be glad therefore to make any conditions with her. But a woman of prudence will know when she is well; will take no such precipitate steps; but will rejoice in the discovery of her husband's great affection towards her, as a means for pursuing the course of Teasing and Tormenting, which I here recommend.

'Oh the joy it is to have a good servant,' cried Sophronia, who had not goodness of heart enough to be kind to any human creature, and whose joy must therefore arise from having a proper subject to torment! But with what ecstasy then, might the artful Livia cry out—'Oh the joy it is to have a good husband!'

If you bring a large fortune to your husband, custom and example will justify you in being as insolent as you please. Solomon himself bears testimony to the intolerable yoke a man takes upon his neck, who submits to be supported by his wife.* But my advice is, that if you bring no fortune to your husband, you should be as insolent as if you had increased his store by thousands. This, I own, is a bold stroke; but does not want its precedents.

If a man marries you without a fortune, and raises you, perhaps, many degrees from the state to which you was born, is it not for his honour, that you should show him that your spirit can rise with your fortune? In what can a woman show her spirit more, than in insolence and opposition? for are ye not taught from your cradles, that submission and acquiescence is *meanness*, and unbecoming a woman of spirit? Not but you may insult your husband frequently with the words duty and obedience,

---

[1] Ecclesiasticus 25: 22.*

provided you never are *mean* enough to bring them into your practice.

If the fortune (as before observed) be entirely on your husband's side, you may also be pretty sure of the strength of his affection towards you, as that alone could determine his choice; and therefore you have the firmest foundation to work upon. There is, besides, another deep malignant pleasure, that must arise in the breast of every woman that makes a vexatious and tormenting wife, to a man who has generously lifted her from distress and obscurity, into affluence and splendour; I mean, the hope that her example will deter many a man from conferring the like obligation. This, I confess, may save some men from being plagued with a termagant; but I rather believe, that it will prevent many a good girl's happiness; as also the happiness of every generous man, who is thus scared from attempting the likeliest method (if there be such a thing as gratitude in a female breast) for conjugal felicity.

If your husband is not a man of an independent fortune, but is in any trade or profession; if also he should have met with misfortunes and rubs* enough to have kept him back from the high road to riches, be sure to show such a despondency towards every scheme or step he takes for the advancement of his fortune, as will sink and depress his spirits, and render him fearful of the event of almost every undertaking. Add also your earnest advice, against every proposal he makes. By this means, you will hang such a weight on him, that he will have no enjoyment of his life. Should his schemes and endeavours succeed, you may enjoy the fruits of his industry, and find other ways enough to plague him. But should they fail, let him not want the additional load of your reproaches for not having followed your advice; and you may lament as loudly as you please, for your poor self, and your poor children. Say boldly to him, 'See, barbarous man, how, by your misconduct, *you* have ruined *my* children.' For you must seem absolutely to forget, that your husband has any share in your mutual offspring, although you see him pierced with the most poignant affliction by his fears for their future welfare. And in this, custom will countenance you enough to take off all fear of censure from the world for such a practice.

If you marry a widower with children, I would rather advise you to consider those children as a means put into your hands to plague your husband, than as new subjects for you to torment.

If you yourself are a widow, the well-known path lies before you, of insulting, plaguing, and tormenting your second husband by praises of your first. And this practice is so well-established, that we have an old saw,* which advises no man to marry a widow, unless her first husband was hanged.

A woman, by her profligate behaviour, may bring infamy on herself and her husband: by her extravagance, she may attempt to ruin him: or by a violent termagancy of temper, she may never suffer him to have a moment's peace or quiet in his house. But these enormities, it is presumed, will render her detestable in the eyes of the world, and may put her husband on some measures of redress. Her extravagance with some difficulty may be restrained; for her scandalous intrigues, a divorce from her may be obtained; and if a man finds perpetual storms and ill humour at home, he is at liberty to fly from so hateful a place. Such violent measures therefore, as I have the highest regard to the reputation of my pupils, I absolutely forbid. It is your delicate strokes I recommend, and those must come from pretended fondness.

You may complain of every hour your husband spends from you with any of his friends, as robbing you of his dear company. You may frequently repeat the following fond speech mentioned in the Spectator, 'You are all the world to me; and why should not I be all the world to you?'*

Be sure not to like or approve of any of your husband's friends; and, when in company with them, say so many half-rude things, as will keep him in a continual fright for you; and will make him hasten them away as soon after dinner as possible, to prevent your exposing yourself; and, perhaps, exposing him to a quarrel, in order to support your ill manners. As soon as your husband returns home, you may fall on his friends for taking him away from you; and abuse them with all the virulence you are mistress of. But should you have indulged yourself in railing at them, and have said so many bitter things against them, as to have grated your husband's soul, and to have raised in him a little degree of anger, you have nothing to do but to own yourself* a weak, silly, fond woman, apt, you may confess, to take prejudices, nay, aversions, to those who would endeavour to share with you the least portion of your husband's affections. Then, bursting into tears, you may add, that nothing but the most hard-hearted wretch in the world could be angry with his poor wife, for hating anybody out of love to him; but you *did* and *would* hate and detest them all, as long as you lived. On this your husband will be forced to sue for reconcilement; which you must by no means grant, till you have brought him to acknowledge, that the highest mark of affection you can show towards him, is to hate and abhor all those whom he esteems and loves.

This behaviour, even towards his men friends, will pass for love; but, as to all his female acquaintance, you need not fear showing the highest degree of jealousy towards every woman he speaks to: nay, you may, to show your extravagant fondness for him, watch his very eyes in company, and fail not to upbraid him with unkindness, for looking at any woman besides yourself. Let a smart curtain-lecture* also be the certain consequence of his having spoke, with the least degree of praise or approbation, of any woman whatsoever. These practices must be where you know they will tease, and where, also, you have not any real cause for jealousy. But should you have reason to think, that your husband is false to you, it is a very nice* point: I have heard of wives, who, by a seeming blindness to their husbands' inconstancy, and by a double portion of cheerfulness and good humour, have recalled their wandering affections: the husband also, by this amiable behaviour in his wife, like a man near shipwrecked in the stormy seas, has been so enamoured of his native home, as never more to quit so happy an asylum as the kind bosom of such a wife. This method, it is true, recalls the husband (if he is worth recalling); but it makes him blessed; and is, therefore, unfit for the practice of my pupils. The man in our case likewise, if possible, must be recalled and got into trammels; for which reason, open rage and resentment against him for his inconstancy must be suppressed, as it might drive him from the company of his cross wife to the arms of his kind mistress. However, I think you may venture to throw forth as much rage and venom as you please against the hated strumpet who has deprived you of your lawful property. You may excuse your husband, by inveighing against the cunning arts of bad women, who make it their business to draw aside easy-tempered, unwary men. You may declare your fondness so great for dear Billy, that you can forgive *him* anything, although you are determined, if possible, to stab or poison the base wanton harlot who seduced him from your lawful bed: then, casting your fond arms about his neck, you may utter such a mixture of feigned love, and real reproaches, as will entangle him too strongly to make him break from you, and yet will make him wish himself surrounded with a swarm of hornets, rather than encircled with such tormenting endearments.

If your husband has sisters, and is fond of them, study every art of behaviour towards them, that will plague and vex *him*. Be sometimes over-civil and formal to them; at other times perfectly rude, insolent, and ill-bred: but never leave, till you have, by some means or other, entirely alienated your husband's affections from them. Then change your views, and consider *them* as new subjects of your own power; practise every art of Teasing and Tormenting towards them; and your husband also (if he is under proper management, and you have a due influence over him) will join with you in the sport: and unless they, by some means of independence, escape your power, you cannot well have better game.

When a man has married a real gentle-spirited, good woman, I have sometimes seen the husband's sisters attempting this sort of pastime with her, but, generally, with very ill success; unless the husband be of so mighty uncommon a temper, as to suffer any woman, who is *not* his bedfellow, to have the least ascendancy over him: but these cases are so very rare, that I cannot help advising my pupils, whose brothers are married, not to show their teeth, where they are so little likely to bite; but rather to wait, till they themselves can be so happy as to get a man on their side, who will support them in all their tricks and insolence.

Besides nourishing in your mind an inveterate hatred against all your husband's relations and acquaintance, you may show the highest dislike to every place he was fond of before he married: but express the highest joy and raptures on the very mention of any place, that you used to live in yourself before your union with him;* and be as lavish as possible of your praises of a single life. You may also, if your husband be not of a very jealous temper, hoard up a parcel of favourite trinkets, as rings, snuff-boxes, &c. which were given you before marriage; and let it appear, from your immoderate fondness for those baubles, that the givers of them are still nearest to your heart.

Carefully study your husband's temper, and find out what he likes, in order never to do any one thing that will please him.

If he expresses his approbation of the domestic qualities of a wife; such as family economy, and that old-fashioned female employment, the needle; neglect your family as much as ever his temper will bear; and always have your white gloves on your hands. Tell him, that every woman of spirit ought to hate and despise a man who could insist on his wife's being a family drudge; and declare, that you will not submit to be a cook and a seamstress to any man. But if he loves company, and cheerful parties of pleasure, and would willingly have you always with him, insult* him with your great love of needlework and house-wifery. Or should he be a man of genius, and should employ his leisure hours in writing, be sure to show a tasteless indifference to everything he shows you of his own. The same indifference, also, may you put on, if he should be a man who loves reading, and is of so communicative a disposition, as to take delight in reading to you any of our best and most entertaining authors. If, for instance, he desires you to hear one of Shakespeare's plays, you may give him perpetual interruptions, by sometimes going out of the room, sometimes ringing the bell to give orders for what cannot be wanted till the next day; at other times taking notice (if your children are in the room), that Molly's cap is awry, or that Jacky looks pale; and then begin questioning the child, whether he has done anything to make himself sick. If you have needle-work in your hands, you may be so busy in cutting out, and measuring one part with another, that it will plainly appear to your husband, that you mind not one word he reads. If all this teases him enough to make him call on you for your attention, you may say, that indeed you have other things to mind besides poetry; and if he was uneasy at your taking care of your family and children, and mending *his* shirts, you wished he had a learned wife; and then he would soon see himself in a jail, and his family in rags. Fail not to be as eloquent as possible on this subject, for I could bring you numberless precedents of silly and illiterate wives, who have half talked their husbands to death, in exclaiming against the loquacity of *all* women, who have any share of understanding or knowledge.

If your husband should be a musical man, you will have many opportunities of teasing and plaguing him. Frequent interruptions and noises, by yourself or children, may be played off upon him; and you must take such an aversion to the sound of all musical instruments, and to all the tribe of fiddlers (as you may call them), that your husband, wearied out by your clamour, may, possibly, give up his favourite amusement. But should you not have power enough over him to carry your point in that manner, you have nothing for it but the old trick of indifference, and sullen dislike, both to his own performance in music, and to any collection of hands by which he might hope to give you some entertainment.

Be out of humour when your husband brings company home: be angry, if he goes abroad without you; and troublesome, if he takes you with him.

If your husband be a real domestic man; if he takes delight in his own family, and the company of his wife and children; then be sure never to be easy in your own house; but let visiting, plays, operas, Vauxhall, Ranelagh,* &c. be your chief delight. The least restraint from any of these gives you a fair opportunity for pouts or wrangling; and you will also have the whole sex on your side, against the barbarous man who should deny his poor wife the free enjoyment of such innocent amusements.

If your husband should be willing either to stay at home, to go abroad, or to lead any kind of life that would be most agreeable to you, never let him find out what *would* be most agreeable to you:

this may be done either by a childish pettishness, and wayward ill humour with everything he proposes, or by a mock compliance: for when he says, 'Would you like, my dear, to do so, or so?' you may answer, 'Let it be just what you like, Mr B——; for you know I never dispute your will.'

If your husband, on observing you particularly fond of something at a friend's table, should desire you to get it for yourself at home, you may say that you are so little selfish that you cannot bear to provide anything for your own eating; and this you may boldly declare, although it should be your common practice to provide some delicacy for yourself every day. It is most likely, that your husband will let this pass; but if he should not, you may, on detection, fly to tears, and complaints of his cruelty and barbarity, in upbraiding you with so small an indulgence as that of a chicken, or a tart, sometimes, for your own eating, when he knows that your weak stomach will not give you leave to make the horse-like meals that he does.

If you manage this scene rightly, and sufficiently reiterate in your husband's ears the words cruel, unkind, barbarous, &c. he will, it is most likely, forget the true occasion of all this uproar; will begin to think he had been a little hard upon you in taking notice of a daily indulgence, which he himself had not only allowed, but requested you to accept; he will ask your pardon, and confess himself in fault, doubling his diligence for the future, in providing all sorts of rarities to gratify your palate.

Be it observed, that this knack of turning the tables, and forcing the offended person to ask pardon of the first aggressor, is one of the most ingenious strokes of our art, and may be practised in every connection, where the power is founded in love.

But to return:

Should your husband, instead of desiring you to please yourself, provide something for you without your knowledge (as many kind husbands have done) in order to give you a small unexpected pleasure, then be sure not to touch a mouthful of it; and, if your circumstances are but low, you may upbraid him with his extravagance for buying what he can so little afford.

This cannot easily be practised in high life, where all sorts of

elegancies and rarities are every day provided; but still, if you
have a fond husband, you may, in the midst of the highest plenty,
give him no small uneasiness, even in this article of eating, by
never letting him see you swallow half enough, to keep body and
soul together. But do not mistake me in this point, and really
starve yourself to vex your husband: for if you have a trusty
Abigail, she will daily bring you up, into your own dressing-
room, a boiled chicken, a roasted sweetbread, or any other thing
you like; and there are ways enough from your own private purse
to bribe her to secrecy.

When your husband is absent, insist so strongly on a letter
from him every post, that he shall often be put to the highest
inconvenience to write, or will suffer great uneasiness from the
thought of your being disappointed. The very first time you
receive not the expected letter, make no allowances for the carelessness of servants, who carry letters to the post-house, or for
twenty trifling incidents that may be the cause of your disappointment; but *say* that you are sure some dreadful accident has
happened. Then immediately hire a man and horse, and send
him, if it be two hundred miles, to enquire after your dear husband's health; or you may get into a post-chaise,* and go yourself.
But should your worldly circumstances be such, as not to be in
the least hurt by this expensive messenger; or should your husband be so situated, that your coming to him would be neither
very perplexing or inconvenient, then hire no such messenger;
take no such journey; but stay and enjoy yourself in the place you
are in; only fail not to write to him such a letter, as will heartily
vex him, and keep him upon the fret, with the thoughts of your
uneasiness (whilst you are very cheerful and merry) till a post or
two will clear up the matter to him, and he, poor man, is at last
satisfied, that you are no longer miserable with your fears for his
health and safety.

This practice of letter-writing, if properly managed, is one of
the most fruitful branches of our trade; but seems too well-
known, to need more than this short hint upon that subject.

When your husband is from home (but not far distant),
although you should be in ever so good health, in ever so high

spirits, and should be enjoying yourself, in his absence, with a set of your own friends and acquaintance; yet the very instant he appears, throw a languidness into your countenance; let your voice grow small; complain of every ailment incident to the human body; and appear so perfectly dejected and low-spirited, that your fond husband will be under the utmost anxiety about you. Instead of finding his own house the seat of joy and gladness, and meeting with a cheerful companion there to heighten his pleasures and alleviate his cares, he will find his own spirits depressed; he will be obliged to stifle every cheerful incident he might have collected for your amusement; he must either give himself up to melancholy and discomfort at home (for your friends, if he stayed, would, on seeing the part you intended to act, soon troop off), or he must seek relief by flight, and associating with his companions abroad. Should the latter be his choice, then the day is your own. You may, the moment his back is turned, resume your spirits, your good humour, your gaiety, and make merry with your friends. You need not blush for the appearance this will make to *them*; for if your visitors are married females, it is ten to one, but they have, some of them, often practised the same themselves. Nor need you be apprehensive of the others for telling tales upon you; even although they should detest your odious pranks; for out of the many hundred (I will not say thousand) husbands, that have been served this trick, I ask if one single one was ever yet informed of this kind of pleasant behaviour in his wife?

CHAPTER III

To the Friend

BEFORE I begin my instructions on this head, it is necessary to say something concerning the article of friendship itself, of which, I think, there are to be found three several sorts.

An ingenious French writer has indeed divided them into many more;* but as they all (except one) come under my second or third head, I shall not in this place follow his division.

The first sort is that real, true, and reciprocal friendship, which was said to subsist between Pylades and Orestes, Castor and Pollux,* and between several others, that are to be found in certain books—and perhaps nowhere else—

The second is that sort of intercourse, where good fellowship, good wine, and a certain sympathetical idleness, draw people together; and in such a society, till they quarrel about some trifle or other, they generally choose to call one another by the name of *Friend*.

The third sort is where one person has a real capacity for the exercise of such friendship, as was shown from Jonathan to David;* and who from a desire of energizing this his favourite affection, has attached himself to an artful cunning man.

It is in this third class alone, that my rules can properly be exercised. To all those therefore, who, by the specious bait of pretended goodness and benevolence, have been so lucky as to have drawn on upon their hook one of these gudgeons,* I shall address the instructions in this chapter.

In the first place, be very careful not to mistake your man. The marks by which you may know your proper dupes are as follow:

An honest, open countenance is a very good sign: for there is much more in physiognomy,* than people generally seem to allow.

If he talks in company greatly in praise of benevolence, good nature, generosity, charity, &c. hold yourself in some doubt of him: but if his praises of the above virtues seldom flow from his mouth, except to commend some living person, who has done a humane or generous action, you may make a farther trial of him. However, don't thoroughly trust him (for all his fine talking), till you can catch him doing such actions himself, as far as is within his power; doing them, also, without ostentation. Then mark him down as your own; and you may make good sport with him, if you rightly understand the game.

There is one mistake which people have often run into, in their choice of a dupe; namely, in thinking that the principal qualification to be insisted on is his having a soft place in his head; whereas the chief thing to seek after is the man who has a soft place in his heart. Many a disappointment has arose, from fixing your choice on a fool; for frequently will you find such a want of affection, such a thorough selfishness, so much cunning and obstinacy, annexed to folly, that all your labour will be thrown away.

The interested use that is to be made of your friends, I shall not here enlarge upon, as there are so many good examples already published, to which I could refer my reader for his practice on that head; particularly the behaviour of Jonathan Wild towards his friend Mr Heartfree.* Besides, in this practice, you can give but one heavy blow; nor is there much scope for continual Teasing and Tormenting, as it is the nature of these generous dupes, while you are ruining them, to be pleased and delighted with their power of serving you. When you have, indeed, entirely ruined them, and openly laugh at them for their silly credulity, they will, on the discovery of your baseness, feel at first a sudden shock, with a sort of rent in their affectionate hearts, for being forced to change friendly love and confidence into distrust and abhorrence: but this, in a gentle mind, will soon subside into resignation (and even compassion to you, for the wretched state of wickedness you are in); and it will never more be in your power to deceive or vex them.

<hr />

[1] *Life of Jonathan Wild.**

The common practice of deserting their friends in distress, men who choose such a proceeding, are already too well-versed in to need my instructions. It is not your obvious or trite practices, but your more refined strokes, that I would wish to point out.

There is also another objection to the absolutely deserting your friends in distress of circumstances; which is as follows: the only pleasure you can propose (you know) from such desertion, is, that your friend may be starved, or reduced to a very abject state: now, in all probability, you will be deceived in your hope; for when people's nearest and best friends desert them, it is very common for them to find assistance from strangers, where they least expected it. Nay, there are some strange people so bent upon defeating the purposes of ungenerous friends or relations, that they will, underhand, without desiring any acknowledgements, without so much as putting it in the power of the obliged to make them any return, send handsome presents to those who are in want:* nor will they give you any clue to guess from whence such bounty comes, unless you happen to know their disposition to be so noble and generous, that you cannot be at a loss to know where your real and grateful thanks are due.

Besides, another strong reason against the absolute desertion of your friends, is that it might make you ill spoken of amongst those who have no notion of any pleasure higher, than that of relieving their friends' distress. I would rather, therefore, advise a method, which would answer the purpose of Tormenting much better; and would, at the same time, gain you the reputation of generosity amongst all those who enquire not beyond the outward appearance of anyone's actions.

If your friend should come to any worldly misfortune, be sure, in the first place, not to fail telling him (and that repeatedly), that it was entirely by his own fault. Then add as many aggravating speeches as you can heap together. Be very lavish to him of your advice to do impossibilities;* but stir not a step for his relief, except he should be so nearly connected to you in blood, that your reputation, as before observed, will suffer by such a total

---

[1] See Mr Orgueil to David Simple, Vol. the last, Bk. VI, ch. 4.*

neglect. In that case, you may either take him into your house (if he will come thither); and let him, according to the old saying, live the life of a toad under a harrow;* or make him some shabby allowance, hardly enough to keep him from starving, but sufficient to prevent his seeking for support from any other means, without risking your displeasure, for not resting satisfied with what you thought a sufficient subsistence.*

As I have the highest regard for the reputation of my pupils, I would, if possible, form all my instructions upon that plan; and have endeavoured, to the utmost, to follow the exemplars they are taken from; who are not the openly cruel and hard-hearted, but rather the specious pretenders to goodness, who, under an outcry about benevolence, hide the most malevolent hearts.

If your own affluence, and your friend's indigence, should ever put it in your power to practise the above rule, it will be as effectual for Tormenting, as any in this collection; not from the obvious reason of your friend's being near starving, or his wanting the necessaries of life; for those inconveniences are trifling, in comparison with the pain and anguish it is to a generous and affectionate mind, to be treated so cruelly and unworthily. To deny a common beggar your bounty which he asks, can only be depriving him of a meal; but to give bountifully to a common beggar, and to deny assistance to your friend, is the highest gratification to a proud and cruel disposition.

Let me add, also, that if it has been in your power to act according to either of the foregoing methods, the more cruelly you have used your friend, the more liberal must you be of your slander and abuse upon him, in order to justify your own proceedings.

To ruin a man by imposing on his generosity and good nature, and then to laugh at him, to insult your distressed friend with reproaches, and to wear away his very soul by insults, under the mask of kindness; may be called the *Racks*, the *Tortures*, of friendship. I shall, therefore, quit such deep proceedings, and come to

---

[1] This exemplified by the author of David Simple, in *Familiar Letters*, vol. i, letter 5, vol. ii, letter 21.*

the lighter, finer strokes, more suited to the directions given in all the other connections. As my instructions, also, have been hitherto chiefly directed to my female readers, I will pursue the same method; especially as there is, in female friendship, a much more intimate connection, and more frequent opportunities of practising the subtle strokes of teasing, than amongst the men. If, therefore, my fair readers will be so good as to adapt the directions for the choice of a friend to their own use, I will beg the men, as far as they can, to adapt to their practice the instructions contained in the remaining part of this chapter.

The natural connection on which to found friendship, seems to be that of having sprung from the same parents, having sucked the same milk, having had the same education, and being joined by interest as well as blood. Some friendships of this kind have been very exemplary: but yet it is so very common for brothers and sisters to fight and scratch when they are children, to live a life of quarrelling and snarling when they are grown up; to hate and envy each other with such inveteracy as admits of no disguise; that it is not to such I address my instructions. However, should two sisters choose to play at friendship with each other,* whilst one of them considers the other as her property or dupe, to such these my rules may be of some service.

When you have fixed on a friend, by the directions already given, endeavour to engage her affections by all the kind and obliging methods you can invent.

When you are very certain, that you are really become the object of her warmest friendly affection, and that her chief joy and pleasure is placed in your company, and in your satisfaction, try how a change of temper will agree with her: grow very melancholy and peevish to everyone around you, except to this friend; but, to her, still express great love and fondness: nay, you may frequently suffer yourself to be talked out of your peevishness and ill humour, by her cheerful endeavours to amuse you. To see this change of temper in you will grieve her to the heart; but still, while she finds it is in her power to relieve your complaints, and to raise your dejected spirits, she will herself, sometimes, feel such an overflowing of joy, as will repay her for any trouble, fatigue, or pain, that she may have undergone. Let her go on some time in this situation; for she will, by her own compassion, entangle herself too strongly ever to break loose from your chains; although you should hereafter treat her with the most barefaced disregard, insolence, and inhumanity.

Prosperity is, indeed, the proper time to exert insolence; but adversity is the time to engage the affections of the tender and compassionate, so as to make your insolence to them in prosperity more sharply felt.

But it is time now to turn the tables; to be extremely cheerful and good-humoured to all around you; and to be melancholy, peevish, and ill-humoured, only with your friend.

Make your company so unpleasant, that she shall have no enjoyment in it; and then perpetually upbraid her with not choosing to be always with you.

As it has been already advised to upbraid people with their real misfortunes, as being their own fault; so do you, on the other hand, if you come to any mishap through your own folly and obstinacy, not believe your own ears or eyes, if your friend is tender and kind to you. What I mean is this.—If she will not take the part of one of my scholars, by adding affliction to the afflicted; do you say to her that, for all her frequent visits, and kind words, yet you know that, in her heart, she does not pity you; because she thinks your misfortunes are owing to your own misconduct. Then begin to rail most vehemently at the hard-heartedness of the world, the cruelty of *all* friends; and you must obstinately refuse to be comforted with her utmost endeavours to please and comfort you.

Tell your friend all sorts of spiteful stories, that you have heard concerning her; by which means you may vent your own spleen, and yet hide the rancour of your intention, under the pretence of disbelieving all such calumny; railing, also, at the ill nature of the wicked, censorious world you live in.

It has ever been held a part of friendship, for friends to tell each other, in a gentle manner, of those faults which it is in their power to rectify. You also, my good pupil, may tell your friend, not only of every fault, but of every human frailty she happens to have: but, be sure, let it not be in an obliging or tender manner. Let it be the effect of some sudden displeasure against her; and you may take that opportunity, also, of telling her as many shocking truths, exaggerated by unkindness, as you can possibly muster up. Should she remonstrate or complain of your unkind words, you must give her this answer, that, truly, you could not, nor would, flatter anyone.

For remember, that flattery is only to be used in order to draw somebody in, on whom you may exercise the utmost brutality, under the name of plain-dealing.

Never mind whether your friend has really any faults or not: for you may falsely accuse her of as many as ever you please. Be very liberal of your unjust suspicions, and false accusations; as they are the daggers which give the deepest wounds from the hand of a friend. Let not a twenty years experience of the truth and fidelity of your friend prevent your loading her with the most unjust suspicions, and accusing her with thoughts and designs towards you, of which you either do know, or, at least, ought to know, that she is perfectly incapable. This is most nobly grating to a generous mind: for truly is it said, that *those injuries go nearest to us, that we neither deserve nor expect.*

It is very possible to hurt your friend by an extravagant overstrained commendation of some person or other for some particular good quality which you have lately been pleased to accuse her with the want of: but take care that your accusation was a false one, or else the whole joke will be lost.

When you have exhausted all your stock of suspicions, accusations, &c. against your friend, or have a mind for a little variety in your practice, there is no better sport, than to abuse every creature that you know your friend has any regard for: but measure out such abuse in its due proportion; namely, give the greatest share to that person or persons whom you know to be most esteemed by your friend.

When you see your domestics very ready to observe your commands, it is no uncommon way, to complain that you can get nothing done, unless you do it yourself. But as servants generally regard not such sayings, and often laugh at your anger and peevishness behind your back, it would be much better to say this to a friend, whom you see very assiduous to do everything in her power to serve you.

When a person so thoroughly loves his friend that it is one of his greatest pleasures to serve, to please, or to amuse him; he cannot, it is true, want thanks for everything he does; nay, he will be so far from it, that nothing could be more unpleasant to him, than to receive such perpetual acknowledgements for his kindness: yet there is a manner of overlooking such constant endeavours, which is not only mortifying, but very grating, and which I would have you, my good pupil, not fail to practise. But if ever it has been in your power to do the least service to your friend, you may puff and blow; you may magnify the trouble you have taken; and you may praise your own friendly disposition and good nature, till you have forced from your friend thanks and acknowledgements enough to repay you for having conferred the greatest favour in the world.

Should you also have desired your friend to transact some affair for you, and she, notwithstanding her utmost care and diligence, should fail in her negotiations; do you not fail to blame her for the faults of others; and say, that you know it was all owing to some neglect in her, and her want of inclination to serve you. Add also, that you would trouble her no more: and here properly will come in your lamentation, that 'you can get nothing done for you, unless you do it yourself.'*

We have an old English proverb (I wish it more delicately expressed) which says, that *proffered service*, &c.* Keep this proverb constantly in your head, and let your friend daily experience the truth of it: for whatever she does to divert, to please, or to serve you, be sure, in the first place, to be neither diverted nor pleased with it; and, in the next place, make out, if possible, that her voluntary endeavours to serve you were of the highest disservice to you. Nay, you may add (if you think she is in a humour to bear it), that you suppose she did this thing with a design to plague, vex, and distress you.

There is a story in *David Simple*, of a man who saved another from drowning; but, in dragging him out of the water, happened to hurt the tip of his ear.* The man, whose life was saved, had by the next day forgot the service that had been done him, and made most heavy complaints about the pain he felt in his ear. The example of this worthy man* may be of great use: for if ever your friends do anything to serve you, never rest till you have found out some omission in them, by which you have suffered some trifling inconvenience. Of this complain most loudly, without ever mentioning one word of the benefit or emolument you may have received.

Should your friend, through neglect or inadvertency, have really done something that was disagreeable or inconvenient to you, for which she is heartily vexed; and therefore, confessing herself in fault, should ask your pardon for it; you may answer, that you very readily forgive her; for it was not your way, to be long angry with your friends. Besides, you may say, that you did not think her half so much to blame, as some *other folks*, by whose example and instigation she used you in this cruel manner. This reproachful pardon will certainly draw some answer from your friend, and you may contrive to keep on bickering on this irksome subject, till you have put her into a passion. Then by your own coolness may you get the better of her, and irritate her on, till you have thrown her so much into the wrong, that she shall again be obliged to ask your pardon; which you may delay or grant, just as you find her temper will bear.

Keep as strong a command over your own passions, I mean those of anger and resentment, as possible. First, that you yourself may never be thrown off your guard; and, next, that you may the better counterfeit those very passions. For it is as true of anger as it is of love, that none can feign it so well, as those who are free from its power.

Great sport may sometimes be made out of a passionate person; but it is like playing with edged tools; they chance now and then to fetch the blood; and you will frequently, as we say, have the worst end of the staff: therefore my advice is, that you choose for your friend a person of a mild and patient disposition; one not easily provoked, nor ever giving way to wrath. You may then safely pretend often, to throw yourself into violent passions. You may accuse the patient sufferer with cunning and art, in putting on a calmness (you may say) only to insult you. Nevertheless you may boldly insult her, with some such words as these: 'I suppose you admire your own wisdom! I suppose you think me a passionate fool, and provoke me in this manner only to expose me!' Thus will you turn the tables, and make her endeavour to soothe you. Nay, if she loves a quiet life, she will, if she finds you will not be pacified without it, ask your pardon, instead of your asking hers for having indulged your own fractiousness and for having abused her for nothing. By this practice you will also have the world on your side, from that favourite maxim (which it is not our interest to contradict), that passionate people are always the best-natured.

There is one precept extremely essential to this art, but of such general use that it is difficult to know under which head to place it; for it equally serves every connection. It has been hinted at in the advice to parents; but, pray, let it not be omitted amongst friends: this is, never to give a kind or cheerful reception to the person who has been some time absent. If the person is any way your dependant, sour looks, and severe reprimands, are proper: but if it is your husband or friend, upbraidings and reproaches for absence will be the most teasing method you can pursue.

There is one circumstance, which may give you a most delightful opportunity of teasing your friend, and which is generally practised in most families, where there are a number of young female friends; I mean where one young lady has a lover.

If you find, that all the coquetry you can exert, that all the arts you can use, to render yourself agreeable, and by that means to rob your friend of her lover, should fail, and he should still remain her admirer, you must comfort yourself for your disappointment, by the following ingenious methods:

You must exert the whole power of what is called raillery on your friend, for every the least additional ornament she bestows on her person, whenever she expects her lover. You must noddle, and laugh, and pretend to be very merry, and tell her how extremely becoming such a ribband* is, and how prettily adapted to her complexion such a coloured gown is; and you may say, 'It is easy to guess, my dear, by your smirking countenance, who is expected today.' As few girls have courage enough to own the truth;* namely, that they really wish to appear as agreeable as they can in the eyes of their lover, your friend will be greatly teased and vexed by this your raillery. Nay, if she happens to have any great degree of bashfulness, she will even omit many points of dress, to avoid your jokes; you may also attack her with all your smartness, on any little effort she makes in conversation, to appear sprightly and agreeable; by which means she will be so much afraid of your raillery, that she will appear to the greatest disadvantage, where she would most wish to please. When you have thus got her down, you may yourself dress out, and talk away, and have one more trial of skill, perhaps, for becoming her rival.

If you know of any little failings she has, which she would wish to conceal (at least, till she had rendered herself, by many real good qualities, so much esteemed by her lover, that if he was a good-natured man, he would forgive them), be sure to bring them all out before him as soon as possible, in hopes of preventing any violent attachment. This has been sometimes practised with success, even among the men; for I once knew a match entirely broken off (and the man was almost distracted for the loss of his mistress) only by his friend's saying to him, before the lady, 'I wish you was hanged, Jack; for you kept me awake all last night by your confounded snoring.'

If your friend should not be quite sure of her lover, but he should be one of those men, who without any positive declaration of love had engaged her by many acts of gallantry, to live in daily hopes of such a declaration; then have you a fine scope for working and teasing her to death, seconding in a manner all his tricks, either by raising those hopes, or alarming her fear. And you will have the rod of mortification so strongly in your hands on that subject, that you will seldom need any other exercise of your power.

Ill health, a weak frame of body, and low spirits, are the unhappy lot of many people; from whence they reasonably claim both favour and indulgence from the good-natured part of mankind: this tempts numbers to affect those ills, in order to claim the same indulgence. The proper use to be made of distinguishing the real sick from the counterfeit, you will find in my general instructions, &c.

If you are blessed with a larger share of health and spirits than your neighbours, be properly insolent thereon (for people may be health-proud, as well as purse-proud); and you may frequently declare, that you do not believe, that ill health comes to anyone, but through their own self-indulgence. This will do very well amongst all your acquaintance; but will be better towards your friend, if she should be of a weakly constitution; but if she is not, then you had better take the part yourself of affected weakness; as many emoluments may arise therefrom.

There are two ways of plaguing your friends by your requests to them, very different in themselves; but both of excellent use; and are as follow:

If your friend be of such an obliging, complying temper, as to be unwilling to deny you anything you ask; and perfectly averse, also, to contradicting any proposal that would give you pleasure; you may, in the first place, make all sorts of preposterous requests to her; nor value how many absurd and improper things you make her do, in compliance with your whims. In the next place, you must study her temper, to find out what is agreeable or disagreeable to her: then persecute her daily, with proposals to do something or other, that is highly unpleasant to her; by which means she must either live an uncomfortable life, from never doing anything she likes; or she must be eternally contradicting your proposals, and refusing your requests; which may, perhaps, be more irksome to her, than any disagreeable thing you can desire her to do.

The other method of requests is this:

If your friend be so assiduous to serve and please you, that, by making your concerns her own, she, as much as possible, prevents even your very wishes, you may often make such ungracious and disobliging requests, as will be truly grating to a friendly disposition. This is a very refined stroke, and great part of its force lies in the manner of wording your requests, and the tone of your voice in expressing such your desires. There is an honest earnestness, with which people may, sometimes, remind their friends, either of their intentions, or promises, to serve them; and there is a manner of requesting, which carries with it neither insult nor suspicion. But, drawing up your head very high, you must begin your requests thus:—'Let me beseech you—Let me entreat you—Pray do me the favour—I beg you would not forget me so much, as to neglect doing so or so, &c.' To which, if your friend (a little hurt) should tell you, that it was somewhat unkind in you to ask her, _in such a manner_, to do what you was convinced she intended to do without any asking at all; then may you lie snug, and, some time after, play her a most noble backstroke;* for when next you want her to serve you in something which it is impossible for her to guess at without being told, you must omit asking her to do it, or giving her the least hint of the matter: now make up some heavy inconvenience that you have sustained; complain of your great hardship, in not having the advantage of the common assistance of friendship where it is most wanted, from that strange oddness in your friend's temper, that she would _never_ be asked to do anything, without growing angry, and putting herself into a violent passion about it. You may say, also, that, for your part, all you wished was that your friend would tell you how you could oblige her; and you would fly to the Indies to do her any service. Then add as many more warm professions of friendship (as they are called) as you please. This, in all probability, will have a good chance for turning the tables, for making her ask _your_ pardon; and she will, most likely, comply with any terms you shall make, rather than see you uneasy.

If this friend, or property of yours, should happen to have any other connections, you must endeavour to embarrass her as much as possible: for, if she tells you that she is to do such a thing to serve one person, such a thing to oblige another, be sure to make some direct opposite request; so that she shall be certain of disobliging either you, or somebody else.

If it should be in your power to do this friend of yours any service, and she should ever make any requests to you, be very sparing of absolutely denying such requests, for fear of giving her an open cause of complaint against you: but grant all such favours in such a disobliging and ungracious manner, as shall destroy all the pleasure of your friend.

This method of granting favours in a disgustful manner, is one of our chief springs, and must be practised in as many connections as you possibly can introduce it.

But in this, generally, granting your friend's requests, mistake me not so far, as to do her any very essential service; especially such a one as might raise her in rank or fortune, above yourself; for to see one's dearest friend get the start of one in anything, is too much for such friendship to bear. Therefore, rather lose your friend by a refusal, than undergo the above-mentioned horrid mortification.

You need not be at the trouble of racking your invention for spiteful things to say, in order to vex all your acquaintance and friends; for if you will only be sure never to suppress any one thing that comes uppermost, I'll engage (if you are a true scholar of mind) the business will be very completely done.

The affecting low spirits and dejection, in order to afflict your friend, has been already advised; but the affectation of very high spirits is no unpleasant conceit, when you have worked your friends to oil;* or, as Shakespeare says, *Fool'd them to the top of their bent.**

Although you are to vex, plague, and abuse your friends, as much as ever the power you have over them, by their affections, will bear; yet be sure to seem very jealous of any other person's using them ill: this makes the appearance of great zeal for their service; and (blinded by their love for you) they will almost persuade themselves, that it is impossible for you to use them cruelly, when you are so alarmed for fear of their suffering any ill-treatment from another.

In like manner, when you have been harassing a servant all day off his legs, you may pity the poor fellow so extremely, and be so very sparing of his labour, that you will not suffer him to go three steps on a necessary errand for your *friend*, for fear of over-fatiguing him.

Should the person on whom you have practised all the subtle arts of teasing that I have taught, or you can invent, seldom dispute anything with you,* never find any fault with you, nor ever remonstrate against your unkind, your disobliging, and your disagreeable ways, set this down to the account of your own goodness and perfection, and not to the patient forbearance of your friend. Yet you may boldly act in consequence of knowing the latter to be the truth of the case, by continuing and persisting in such a teasing and tormenting behaviour, as little less than the patience of Job* could bear with or endure.

In short, my good pupils, if you study well my instructions; and, from these my outlines, finish for yourselves a complete system for the practice of tormenting your friends; I will be bold to pronounce of you, what Claudian has already so well expressed to my hands,

> *Talem progenies hominum si prisca tulisset,*
> *Pirithoum fugeret Theseus: offensus Orestem*
> *Desereret Pylades, odisset Castora Pollux.**
>
> *Rufinus*, i. 106–8

CHAPTER IV

To your Good Sort of People; being an appendage to the foregoing chapter

SAYS Dean Swift, in his poem of Cadenus and Vanessa,

> *'Tis an old Maxim in the schools,*
> *That vanity's the food of fools:*
> *Yet, now and then, your men of wit*
> *Will condescend to take a bit.**

And may we not, with some propriety, apply this to our ingenious art of Tormenting?

It is acknowledged, that the chief adepts to our science are those only who are blessed with a proper share of spite and malignity: yet, observation has taught me, that many a good man, and many a good woman, who have possessed numberless virtues, have, now and then, recreated their spirits with a small touch of this pleasant sport: and although they have not absolutely inflicted a strong Torment, yet have gone so far in the art of Teasing, as greatly to perplex and disconcert the best-laid intentions for giving them pleasure.

An obliging, complying temper, as shown in the last chapter, may be finely worked and teased, by being forced either to do what is disagreeable, or to be always saying *no*: but the same temper and disposition, by never saying *no*, may very much distress others, as well as itself. To explain my meaning, take two or three short stories; and then, gentle reader, you will be the best judge of the justice of this observation.

What gave me the hint for these kind of reflections, was the account which a young lady (whom I will call Felicia) was giving me of her friend Hermia; who, she said, was the best woman in the world, but, from too great a compliance in her temper, was perpetually falling into inconveniences herself, and making all her friends around her miserable.

'Hermia', said Felicia, 'is a woman whom I love and esteem as my own soul. Her real charity, her benevolence, her gentleness of disposition, show me, that there is at least one human being, in whom every human virtue is centred. So thoroughly am I blessed by the warmth of her friendship, and the kindness of her heart, that I should pronounce myself a monster of ingratitude, if I could move or act with any view but for her pleasure. Her greatest delight is pleasing and obliging all her friends; but, from an unwillingness to give trouble, she never requests any person to do any one thing in the world for her; fearing, I believe, that she should rob her friends of some pleasure of their own. Yet, as it is impossible to know her whole mind so well as she knows it herself, there must, sometimes, be such omissions to her, as will put her to inconvenience, and grieve her friends to behold.

'In the beginning of our acquaintance, this passive disposition of my friend Hermia often gave me great pain: for as she is so very averse to contradicting any proposal, that she will do a thing the most contrary to her own inclinations, rather than thwart another's, I have frequently found myself the cause of giving her great uneasiness,* when it has been the farthest from my inclinations so to do.

'Hermia is far from being of a weakly constitution, but has very strange disorders in her head, for which she is advised to walk long walks; and this, from her good health in all other respects, she is very well able to perform. We were one day, in the country, to walk (in very hot weather) home to her own house, and the distance was about four miles. We were setting out while the sun was yet very high; on which I proposed to her (fearing, indeed, that the scorching heat would hurt her head) to stay till the cool of the evening. I observed to her, also, how beautiful the moon, being that night at the full, would look through the high trees, and in the clear river by whose banks we were to pass. Hermia made not the least objection, but readily consented; and we had, to me, a most agreeable and pleasant walk; nor did she seem less delighted with the various beauties of this rural scene, than myself. But, as soon as she came into the house, she was very much disordered, and really ready to faint away: seeing me excessively concerned, she told me her complaint would soon go off; for it was only the common effect of walking in the moon-light. "It was for that reason", added she, "that I was desirous of walking in the middle of the day; and, indeed, should have done so, if you, Felicia, had not proposed staying till the cool of the evening." I gently complained of her compliance with any pro-posal of mine, in a case where her own health was concerned; and she candidly acknowledged herself to blame. She promised, also, to speak her mind more freely another time. But, before our discourse was ended, she called for some water to drink; and a bottle of wine standing by, I desired her to pour a little into the water, as I feared she was too warm with her walk, to venture on so cool a liquor as water just come from the pump. She readily took my advice, filled the glass half full of wine, drank it off, and in less than five minutes fell into a strong convulsion-fit. I was half at my wit's end. I sent for her physician, and he, on seeing Hermia, asked if she had not tasted some wine, which, he said, always threw her into these kinds of fit. With pain and anguish I replied, that she had drunk a large glass of wine and water, and that I had given it her. It was some hours before she could be brought to her senses. From that day, I attempted not any more to complain; for I found how much in vain it was for me to remon-strate against this her cruel proceeding towards herself, nor was there any way left for me, but by a constant observance and watchfulness to prevent her hurting her own health, in order to oblige others.'

The good-natured Felicia told several more instances of the same kind, expressing the most anxious concern for her friend Hermia's sufferings, on account of that over-compliance and obligingness of disposition, of which she was possessed. But let me whisper it into my friend Hermia's ear, that, notwithstanding the amiable character given of her by her tender friend Felicia, I think I spy in her some marks of a love to our sport.* If it was possible, that the moonlight walk was taken, and the wine was drunk, on purpose to give anxiety to Felicia, I could do no other than pronounce Hermia to be one of my very best pupils—To be got even amongst that upper class of those, who are capable of hanging themselves to spite their neighbours. But as I have reason to believe, that she really deserves the other part of the character given her by Felicia, and that she indulges her own compliance of disposition, to the distress of herself, and all around her, through a thoughtlessness of the consequence of her own actions, I readily dismiss her from my upper class: but I still insist upon it, that she ignorantly fights under my banner, and is one of the flying squadron,* for whose honour and service this chapter is intended.

Hermia, by the male part of my readers, perhaps, may be presumed (as she is a woman) to be weak, and not capable of considering the force of her own words, or the consequences of her own actions: but what shall we say to Albertus?

Albertus is a man of great sense, an uncommon genius, and so very mild and gentle in his disposition, that happy are all those who are nearly connected with him. To enumerate all his real good qualities would (with as much truth as ever it was said) swell this volume to a folio.* He has a friend, Horatio, who has the highest veneration, and the justest regard for him; whose chief delight is in his company; and whose greatest pleasure would be that of being able, by any means, to add to the ease and satisfaction of his friend. But Horatio, like poor Felicia, is perpetually mortified by finding himself in some way or other the cause, the unhappy undesigning cause, of Albertus's distress.

One day, seeing Albertus ill, and hearing him say, that he must be in the city the next morning on very important business, Horatio asked him if he could not commission him to transact this business for him. Albertus thanked him; but said, he feared it might prevent some business or pleasure of his own. Horatio assured him he had no business of his own that day, nor any pleasure, but an invitation to a morning concert, which was an engagement too trifling for him to put in competition with being of any service to his most distant acquaintance, and much more so with his best friend: he begged, therefore, that Albertus would inform him of the business.

Albertus hesitated some time; then said, that he had recollected some circumstances, which made it impossible for anyone but himself to transact the affair; and he must therefore either go himself, or put it off till another day, when he was in better health.

Horatio knowing the sincerity of his own intentions to serve his friend, and not doubting that Albertus, from long experience, knew it as well as himself (having also no desire of making a show of overstrained importunity, where he thought his offer could not be accepted), took his leave, wishing him health to transact his business, and success in the execution of it. Albertus, with great seeming good humour, returned his good wishes, by hoping he would have much pleasure in his musical entertainments.

The next day, Horatio goes to the concert in the morning, and visits his friend in the afternoon. He finds him a little mended in his health; but appearing under great vexation of mind. He hastily and anxiously enquires the cause of his distress. Albertus answers, that he had not been in health or spirits, that morning, to go into the city; that he had sent a man to transact the business for him, and by the blunder of that man he had lost two hundred pounds.

'Since you found it was possible for another to transact your business for you, why, my good friend,' cries Horatio, 'would you not send for me?'

Albertus mildly answers, 'You was engaged, sir, at a concert— you are very fond of music—I cannot bear, for my own convenience, to debar my friends of their *pleasures*.'

Oh Albertus, Albertus, honestly answer me this question. If you believed your friend's regard for you sincere, was you not robbing him of his greatest pleasure, by refusing him an opportunity of doing you an essential service?

It must be confessed, that it is not consistent with the characters to whom this chapter is addressed, to say grating or ill-natured things, with a design to torment; nor can they, by any means, be supposed to feign sickness, or low spirits, for the above-mentioned purpose. But (countenanced by custom) they may, if they please, when they are really sick or low-spirited, indulge the highest degree of fretfulness, peevishness, and ill humour; and may also, from a thorough carelessness of their words and expressions, give some very good random shots, without positively taking aim.

A habit of saying fretful things, without strictly examining into the truth of them, will bring a person into a belief of their reality. As for instance: If you frequently say, that nobody cares for you, it will not be long before you will imagine all mankind your enemies: or if any person should once or twice make you wait, should miss an appointment, or the like, by telling them that they *always* do so, you may work yourself into such a belief of its truth, that a repeated behaviour to the contrary can with difficulty bring you to acknowledge, and be convinced of, your mistake.

Whilst your good sort of people take the allowance that is given to the sick, of indulging every captious and peevish humour that will rise, or attempt to rise, in almost every mind; it is not from such, that I fear the overthrow of our art. But the person uniformly cautious, both in words and actions, never to give the least offence, is our greatest and most powerful enemy. And that we have some such enemies abroad, experience has taught me to confess.

Nay, what a strange creature did I once hear of! A young lady of title and fortune, who had servants, friends, and dependants, at her command, was afflicted with a painful disorder (which at last deprived her of life) for near twelve years; yet never took the opportunity of one of those advantages, to say a cross or fretful thing to anyone! Though born to a high station, she chose a private life; the influence of her example, therefore, was not to be greatly dreaded. But what shall we say, if such a behaviour should even now shine forth, not far from a throne? If there should now be a living example of a person,* that, with as much exterior power as anyone can possess, next to our Sovereign himself, and with as much interior power as the affections of a whole nation can give, never exerts that power, but for the pleasure and benefit, instead of the Torment, of all her dependants: Should we not, my dear pupils, alarmed by the danger of such a shining exemplar, all assemble together, in order, by some envious detraction, to pull down this our greatest enemy? Alas! she is above our reach!

Therefore have we no hope left but in trying to reverse an old general observation, and in arduously endeavouring to show, that these our precepts will be more forcible towards promoting the love of Tormenting, than the most royal and illustrious example will be, towards inculcating and teaching every Christian virtue.

End of Part the Second

General Rules for plaguing all your acquaintance; with the description of a party of pleasure

HE part my pupils are to act in plaguing all their acquaintance could not with any propriety be placed under either of the foregoing divisions: for their power, in this case, arises more from custom and good breeding, than from exterior authority, or affectionate hold of the heart.

Yet, in one sense, it may be said to have a place in each of the foregoing divisions: for there is no better method of plaguing your acquaintance, than so to time the exercise of both your exterior and interior power, as to be insufferably troublesome to all around you.

But, let their methodical place be where they will, my directions are as follow:

As you cannot bind your common acquaintance to you by any of the methods already mentioned, it will be necessary for you to put on such a deportment as will render you, sometimes, very agreeable, in order to prevent your being entirely deserted; except you should happen to be the indulged wife of an uxorious husband, and then you may exert the most barefaced ill humour and insolence that you are capable of; for he must and will support you in all your tricks and impertinence, let them be ever so preposterous and absurd.

By all means avoid an evenness of behaviour. Be, sometimes, extremely glad to see people; and, at other times, let your behaviour be hardly within the rules of good breeding.

If you are acquainted with persons of punctilio,* don't directly affront them; but contrive continually to nettle them, and keep them on the fret, by such a carelessness and neglect, as will take away all their pleasure in conversation: whereas, on the other hand, for that part of your acquaintance who are easy-tempered people, who love civil freedom, and stand not on forms and cere-monies, persecute them with officious complaisance: nor ever let them rest five minutes in the same place; but press them continu-ally to change it for one that you hope is more commodious.

Never let the time of dinner pass in quiet. For if there be not a surly husband to find fault with his wife, and put all the company in pain for her, then let the wife herself find fault with the dress-ing of every dish; send *this* down to be more done; send *that* from the table, for being rotten-roasted; and keep the whole company in such a confusion, as shall at least take away their pleasure, if not their appetites to their dinner.

Suffer your servants to be as negligent, and as rude to your visitors, as they please; nor ever observe whether they give them, at table, clean or dirty glasses, knives, plates, &c. They will undoubtedly be the better to you for this your indulgence in suffering them to plague and insult your friends.

If you lend your coach, wink at* your coachman's insolence or impertinence: for it will save your wheels from being worn out in the service of anyone besides yourself.

There is no better use of having your children noisy and troublesome, than this of plaguing all your acquaintance: for you may suffer them, when you have visitors, to make such a racket that you cannot hear one another speak; let them, also, with their greasy fingers, soil and besmear your visitors' clothes; cut their hoods, capuchins,* or tippets* (if laid in the window), with scissors; put their fingers, and dirty noses (if you are drinking tea), into the cream-pot, and drivel over the sugar; throw the remainder of the cream over somebody's clean gown; climb up upon the chair, and thrust some bread and butter down the ladies' backs;* and, in short, be more troublesome and offensive, than either squirrels, parrots, or monkeys.

You have two ways of acting, on this agreeable behaviour of

---

¹ To avoid the absurdity that must appear in this passage, when the wheel of fashion shall have brought the ladies to dress themselves in the decent manner of their great-grandams; and, by that means, shall have rendered this trick of the child's impracticable; be it noted, that, in the year 1752, it was a general fashion for ladies to appear naked *behind*, almost halfway down their backs.

your children: one is, to put on an absolute blindness, and to take not the least notice of any one enormity they commit: the other is, to find perpetual faults with them before company (if you know they are headstrong enough not to mind you); and, by correcting them for every step they take, you will yourself become as troublesome to your visitors, as the children themselves, without your correction, possibly could be.

If you see people particularly cheerful, rack your invention to the utmost, to find some method of damping their mirth and good humour: for, should you happen to have no friend, husband, &c. in company, on whom to exercise your power; yet, to destroy the mirth of a common acquaintance is some joy, although not the greatest, to a truly malevolent heart.

There are several good tricks of mortification, which you may apply properly, by attending to people's characters and dispositions, so as to find out what they most value and pride themselves upon. Agreeableness, at least, if not beauty of person, is strongly the wish of everyone, even men as well as women; and, from that wish, people are so desirous of believing themselves possessed of it, that personal strokes of mortification seldom miss their aim; although less outward resentment is shown in that, than in any other case.

If Tom Neverout, who dotes on being thought a wit, should look pleased with the approbation of the company for having said a good thing, you may say that a month ago, you heard Jack Jolterhead (whom Tom despises to his soul) say the same thing: on this, the laugh of approbation will be turned into a laugh of contempt, poor Tom will be mortified, and you will be applauded for your wit. Tom will be more inwardly vexed than he will outwardly express, for fear of being again laughed at; and you will have him, all that evening, at your mercy; for you may revive the laugh against him at any time, only by patting him on the shoulder, and saying, 'Come, honest Tom, have you no other good thing of Jack Jolterhead's to pass off for your own, and to divert the company?' This, I have been told, is what they call being smart in company; and, if I might be forgiven the heinous sin of a pun, I should suppose that expression arose from the smarting pain you give to another by this mortifying sort of wit.

To women, your best way is to attack them about their clothes. When you see them pleased with any gown, cap, or ribband, that they have on, you may drop it out (as if by chance), 'that it was exactly such a gown, as you saw Mrs Meagre in at Sadler's Wells;'* carefully remembering, on these occasions, to name either some very frightful, unfashionable, or ridiculous character.

Be continually begging all your acquaintance to help you to servants; to recommend you to manteau-makers,* milliners, with shops of all kinds. The old, experienced ones, who can guess at your intentions by such requests, will decline giving you any such recommendations; but your unexperienced, good-natured people will readily undertake to send you a servant, or to recommend some person in business, hoping, thereby, to please you, and serve and encourage some industrious tradesman. Fail not to employ the person thus recommended: if it is a servant, let him soon be discharged, with great disgrace; nor ever let your friend escape being upbraided with recommending one of the worst of servants. Complain of the manteau-maker, that she spoiled you a suit of clothes, and stole several yards of your silk. If a milliner is recommended to you, you may railly* your friend in the following manner: 'Surely, my dear, you sent Mrs —— the milliner to me out of a joke; for you could not imagine, that I would appear such a *fright*, as that awkward creature, of your recommendation, would have made me!' As to shops of all kinds, you need not buy anything at any place to which you are recommended; but you may complain to your friends, that by their recommendation, you was like to have been cheated most intolerably, had it not been for your own great judgement, by which you plainly perceived, that the person asked double the worth of the goods; and that you could buy them for half the price at any other shop in town.

As the time in which you can exercise your power over a common acquaintance, is no more than a visit will allow; and as that visit, should you grow too troublesome to be endured, can be shortened; your best method would be to propose frequent parties of pleasure; for in such expeditions lies the largest scope for being troublesome; and the company, by this expedient, are in a manner bound together, at least for one day: to this sort of sport, therefore, shall the remainder of this chapter be directed.

In most parties of pleasure, you have commonly one or two, who, by feigned fits, headaches, frights, &c. destroy all the comfort of the day: but, should there be one amongst you, who, from a real weak constitution, is not able to undertake what the healthy part of the company may propose, then postpone those common tricks above to a better opportunity; and fly all at once upon your present game.

Make all sorts of proposals unfit for an unhealthy person to undertake; as walking in the heat of the day, staying out in the damps of the evening, hurrying from one place to another without any respite; or propose any other frolic, to which your invention may help you: if your proposals are complied with, you half kill your victim; but if she should object to these things, you may accuse her of affectation, and a design of spoiling company: or, instead of outward reproaches, you may show, by a sneer, that you do not believe she is ill. You may also say, that you are less able to walk, ride, bear heat, cold, &c. than she is; but, for your part, you do not love giving trouble, nor ever make the least complaint, although you are half dead. But, in this rule, be sure not to mistake your person, and, instead of tormenting a poor sick wretch, detect a true sister of the art: yet such a mistake is not much to be apprehended, as there are as certain marks by which to distinguish a sister of our science, as a brother of the Masonry:* but, far be it from me to divulge these arcana;* I too much revere this our noble art, to expose its inmost mysteries to vulgar eyes. And here give me leave, since I have mentioned Freemasonry, to observe that the practitioners of our art are, I believe, more numerous, than the Masons, and the art itself of still greater antiquity than theirs. They boast their institution but from the tower of Babel,* whereas I doubt not but I could bring proof, that ours is derived from our grand and general mother *Eve* herself.

In all parties of pleasure, the first thing to be considered is, of how much weight and consequence you are to the rest of the company. If you have in the party no husband, lover, or friend, that will indulge or humour you, it is your best way to enjoy yourself as well as you can; only watching for some favourable opportunity, when there is any dispute, so as to put in your opinion on the weakest side; not out of compassion for the weak, but in order by that means to support and increase the wrangle, and to prevent it, for some minutes at least, from coming to an end. But if (as before observed) you have nobody there that will be hurt by your ill humour, don't carry it too far, for fear of being mortified by the contempt of the company; as it would be much better, also, to save it for a more convenient opportunity.

If you know yourself to be of some consequence, although not the very principal person of the party, you may, by opposition, make a good deal of sport. You cannot, indeed, carry things so high, as if you was at the helm; but you may dispute every inch of ground with the queen of the day, provided her forces are not strong enough to render her power absolute. If your party is walking, you must love walking fast, if she happens to like walking leisurely:* in a coach, you must love the glasses* down, and complain of being suffocated, if she chooses them up: in a boat, be the weather ever so fine, you must beg and entreat to have a tilt,* if she likes to be without one: at Vauxhall or Ranelagh, you must be continually teasing the company to go home, if you see them pleased with staying; or you may wait till the proposal is made for going, and, all at once, grow into very high spirits, and complain that they should think of breaking up the party, just as you began to enjoy yourself. In short, keep up in your mind the true spirit of contradiction to everything that is proposed or done; and although, from want of power, you may not be able to exercise tyranny, yet, by the help of perpetual mutiny, you may heartily torment and vex all there that love you; and be as troublesome as an impertinent fly, to those who care not three farthings about you.

If you are the principal person in the party, that is, if you are young and handsome, and have a lover with you; or if you are the adored wife of a man who makes an agreeable party on purpose to please you, consisting of his own sisters, and some other ladies and gentlemen who will acknowledge you are their queen;* then will your reign for that time be absolute; excepting only the quelling, perhaps, a few rebellions which may happen, if you should chance to have any of the above-mentioned mutineers in company.

The power of a beautiful woman over her lover may, perhaps, be greater than that of an indulged wife over her husband; but her power over the rest of the company, for many reasons I could give, cannot be half so great. Take, therefore, the instance of the indulged wife. To such I now address myself; and, to make my instructions clearly understood, let us imagine the party made: let us suppose it to consist of yourself, your fond husband, his two sisters, two young gentlemen, and another young lady. A coach and chaise* (if you have them not of your own) are hired; you, with your husband and his two sisters, go in the coach; the young lady in the chaise, with one of the gentlemen, who we will suppose to be an admirer of hers; and the other gentleman may ride on his own horse. It would be no bad trick, as soon as you are stepping into the coach, to say you are suddenly taken very ill; and so, for that day, disappoint the whole company. But, however, the same party is once more formed; the day is arrived, and you all sally forth, in the same order as before, but not with the same glee; for, after a baulk of this sort, there will always be such a damp on these kind of expeditions, as takes off half their joy. We will suppose your plan to be as follows: you intend to be out three days; to go directly to Windsor, and spend the whole day there; to go the next day to Esher,* in order to see those two beautiful seats, the Duke of Newcastle's, and Mr Pelham's;* to go that night to Hampton Court;* there to discharge your coach, &c. and the next day, after having seen the palace and gardens, to go down the river in a six-oared barge, ordered to meet you there, for that purpose. By this means you enjoy all the beauties of the Thames, with the many fine seats on its banks; and you propose to close your expedition, by calling in the evening both at Ranelagh and Vauxhall.

The weather is fine, and away you go.

When you have travelled about three or four miles, you may

begin to be very uneasy, either with being too hot, or too cold, or just what you please: or you may complain, you are so sick with riding in the coach, that you can go no farther. Should the motion of a coach never before have made you sick, yet you may assert it does so now; for married women have always a pretence for complaining of unaccountable disorders. The whole cavalcade, at your command, will stop; and, for the benefit of more air, you immediately displace the young lady in the chaise, especially if you see her pleased with her situation. This may not be very agreeable to the young gentleman; but, out of complaisance to you, the queen of the party, he will not dispute the exchange. This must not hold long, especially, if passing by, you should hear your husband laughing, or talking in a cheerful manner, in the coach; you must drag him out from thence, but by no means take him into the chaise to you; for then you would leave all the young unmarried folks to themselves: you may plead fear of his driving, and, therefore, beg the young gentleman on horseback to get into the coach, and suffer your husband to ride his horse, that you may have the pleasure of dear Billy's company by the side of the chaise. To this (as it is asked under the mask of fondness) your husband cannot but consent, although he is unfitted by his dress for riding, and perhaps it may also be to him a disagreeable way of travelling. However, as pouts would be the consequence of a refusal, out of the coach he gets, mounts the horse, and rides in the dust to Windsor.

While dinner is getting ready, you walk over the castle; and here you have little to do but to put on an absolute indifference to everything that either your husband, or any of the rest of the company, show you, as being worth your observation. It would be no bad thing, to carry a knotting-bag* with you, and to employ your fingers and attention on that as much as possible, whilst the others are employed in admiring the paintings, and other beauties, of that superb castle. But if either of your husband's sisters should desire you to observe any particular picture, as praising the drawing of it, or taking notice how well it expressed such a piece of history; you may say 'That, indeed, you don't pretend to understand painting and history, and such *learned* things; you leave those studies to such *wise* ladies as they are, who, you suppose, despise you for a weak silly woman.' Although you may just give your sisters one snap, where it lies so fairly in your way; yet, for the most part, by no means seem low-spirited, or out of humour (that does not come in turn yet); but rather hum a tune, and every now and then seem vastly delighted with some trifling thing or other that you meet with, which ought to be below the notice of a girl of eight years old.

At dinner you have nothing to do but to be as troublesome as you can; to dislike everything that is provided, and to send an hundred ways to get something you can eat. If there should be any dish your husband's sisters particularly like, you may hate the smell of it so much, that it must be immediately sent from the table. Should anyone take notice, that you never before disliked the dish; you must boldly declare, that you always hated and abhorred it, and had been ready to faint away twenty times, by its being brought to the table; but nobody had regard enough for you, ever to observe what was agreeable or disagreeable to you in anything. The more false this assertion is, the more likely will you be of carrying your point, that is, of dumbfounding all the company: for should you have eaten very heartily of that very dish but the very day before, it will only strike the company with silent astonishment at your *very* great assurance.

If your husband be a man of taste and relish for fine prospects,* and should have expressed great pleasure, whilst at dinner, with the thought of an evening walk in Windsor Park, and on the terrace; if he should also say to you, 'My dear, I will show you such a view, such a walk, &c.' then lie snug with the thought of playing him a most charming trick, all under the mask of the highest good humour and fondness. For when you are all setting out for your walk on the terrace, and to the park, you may say to your husband, as you lean upon his arm, 'Bid them walk on, my dear, and say you and I will follow them.' Your fond husband, without asking your reasons, will undoubtedly do as you desire, and away they all go. Then do you run back into the room where you dined, call to your husband, and say, 'Come hither, my dear Billy; let you and I stay here and enjoy ourselves, whilst they are

trudging about, and fatiguing themselves in a great wide park.'
Should your husband gently remonstrate, and hint also, how
much pleasanter it would be to walk out, and how much pleasure
he had proposed in showing you the prospects, &c. you may
fondly hang about his neck, and declare, 'that no fine prospect,
nor any other amusement, was any pleasure to you, in comparison
with his dear company: that you preferred that paltry room at an
inn, thus sitting alone with him, before the sight of all the palaces
in Europe; and it would be very unkind in him, if he would not
indulge you in your request of staying there till the company
came in from walking.'* You need not fear carrying your point by
fondling endearments, and trifling good humour. When the company returns from walking, you must seem in the highest spirits
imaginable; and, continuing so all the evening, you may talk in
such a manner of the pleasure you enjoyed in their absence, as
will put your husband in a sweat* for you, and will give the young
fellows an opportunity of putting all the young ladies to the
blush.

This first day of your expedition your husband has been your
chief victim; and that, too, by very little peevishness, but chiefly
by exerting a silly childish good humour.

Now change your method; be very much out of spirits, and
take all occasions of bickering and disputing with your husband's
sisters.

When you arrive at Esher, and you are all going directly to
Claremont,* you may declare that you are not in spirits to walk
about the gardens, and you desire to be left sitting in the house. If
your husband offers to sit with you, tell him 'that you will not on
any account confine him; but you think it would be only common
good manners to you, and good nature to their brother, for his
sisters to offer to stay with you; for it was not very fit you should
be left by yourself.'* On this, it is most likely that one of them will
offer to keep you company. Take not any notice, nor seem the
least pleased with this her civility; but say to your husband, 'that
you are so low-spirited you can enjoy nobody's company; and that
the only thing that could amuse you, would be a game at ombre:*
if therefore he could so far prevail with his sisters, as to persuade

them, once in their lives, to give up their own pleasure for your amusement, you should be glad they would make up your party; but you positively insisted upon it, that you would confine no other part of the company:'* you may add, with a sigh, 'that you hoped, indeed, you might take that small liberty with your husband's sisters.'* Then boldly take the cards and counters out of your knotting-bag; for nobody will dare to tell you, that you put them there for that purpose.

The rest of the company will now have little pleasure in their walk, from this division that you have made; and you must be sure to exert as much spleen and ill humour at cards, as you possibly can: Nor seem to be the least pleased* or obliged by your sisters' compliance with your wayward fancies. You may perpetually tell them, 'that you suppose they wish you hanged, for keeping them from the young fellows;'* with as many other spiteful things as you can invent. You know that, for fear of offending their brother, they will not contradict you; and you may therefore work them within an inch of their lives. If you still continue your low spirits, and pretended fondness for cards, after your husband and the rest of the company are returned from their walk, they will give up all thoughts of seeing Mr Pelham's elegant gardens;* for there can be no enjoyment with such a division of company; and you will in all probability go directly to Hampton Court.

For fear your husband, and the rest of the company, from the damp you have thrown upon their pleasures, should propose returning directly home to London, grow into tolerable spirits, as soon as you come to Hampton Court, and say that you propose great pleasure the next day, in going down the river: you may likewise declare, that Hampton Court Palace was the only place you wanted to see, on account of the beauties there, painted by Sir Godfrey Kneller.*

After you have, by this declaration, prevented the party from being broken up, and your coach, chaise, &c. are all dispatched for London, grow as wayward, fretful, and peevish, as you possibly can; making it the business of the company to endeavour at diverting and amusing you. But be sure to lose this whole day, by coming into no proposal for pleasure; that is, you may put off all their proposals,* by saying you hope to be in better spirits tomorrow. Now is your time to take all opportunities* of showing your power over your husband's sisters; and it would be no bad frolic (by way of making a bustle, and giving them all the plague and trouble you can), if, about an hour after you are abed, you was to declare that you could not sleep in that bed, and so make your husband get up, and prevail with his sisters to change beds with you.

The last day of your expedition is arrived; you walk over Hampton Court Palace, either with some pleasure, or a total indifference, as you showed at Windsor, whichever you like best. The barge is ready, and out you all set, full of the highest joy and good humour. You have a fine day before you; it is agreed that you are to dine at Richmond,* and to walk in the gardens there: then the closing your expedition with Ranelagh and Vauxhall in the evening, gives, in imagination, the highest delight to the younger part of your company; but, in imagination alone, shall they enjoy either that, or Richmond gardens, if you manage right.

Before you reach Kingston,* you may declare that you are suddenly taken with such a panic upon the water as you never felt before;* you may scream at every stroke of the oar; and, in short, when you come to Twickenham,* beg and entreat your husband to let you get out, and travel home by land; for such an unaccountable terror of the water had seized you, that you could not go any farther for the world. Appear so very ill with the fright, that it is proper, at least, for one of your sisters to go ashore with you. But here the fear is, that the rest of the company, being four of them, may pursue their design, and leave you, your husband, and sister, to get home as you can. Give a hint, therefore, to your husband, that, in about an hour, perhaps, when you have drunk a dish of tea with some drops,* you may possibly recover yourself enough to pursue your first design; and, by this means, you may get them all ashore.

Now never leave, till you have set on foot some wrangling dispute or other, that shall sour the whole company, and put them off from every thought of pleasure. It is most likely, that, on this, the young lady whom you the first day turned out of the chaise from her lover, having felt from your wayward humours so many disappointments, and not having the same restraint as your husband's sisters, will make a sort of mutiny, and will rebel against your power: if so, you must exert so much spleen and ill nature towards her, that the young gentleman will not forbear taking her part. Now the sport begins! for she, encouraged by having a knight errant to defend her cause, will grow pretty saucy; and you, knowing your fond husband will support you in it, may increase in your insolence towards her. If you and the young lady are both women of spirit, and the young fellow and your husband are both men of honour, an appointment is made behind Montagu House,* and your party of pleasure ends in a party of tilting;* and like Chevy Chase, 'the child may rue, that is unborn, the *Pleasure* of that day.'*

There yet remain various connections, that give fair opportunities for the exercise of our art; but it is presumed and hoped, that there may be general instructions enough collected from my foregoing principal heads, to make a minute enumeration of every such connection unnecessary. But—

Let all men in power be insolent to their dependants.

Let jail-keepers be cruel to their prisoners.

Let the frequency of corporal punishments, and the infrequency of rewarding men for long and faithful services, show that our science flourishes in military management.

Let the schoolmaster (since nothing lies open to him but the rod) spare not the birch, while custom indulges him in such a smart exercise of his authority.

In all other stations, a sharp and acute wit may, I doubt not, hit on some effectual method, for making somebody or other miserable.

Or, should you be so unfortunate as to have no human creature any way your dependant, you have, at least, the whole race of the domestic brute creation, on whom to wreak your malice.

One subject of your power, indeed, yet remains; and such a one as it is not in the art of man to deprive you of—

I mean *yourself*.—Nor can any rank or degree of men who are my followers supply my train with a larger company than the race of *Self-tormentors*. In this class may be ranked the generality of old bachelors, and old maids; for this very good reason, that they can seldom find any creature who has regard enough for them to be hurt by their ill humour, but *themselves*.

CONCLUSION OF THE ESSAY

THAT great emperor Marcus Antoninus, in those excellent reflections which he has left to the world,* declares that he learned such a precept from one person, and such a precept from another: Give me leave so far to follow his example, as modestly to disclaim the honour of invention in most of the foregoing rules, especially in those which appear the most exquisite and refined; for nothing but experience and observation could have convinced me, that the practice of some of them was possible.

So very delicate is this ingenious art of Tormenting, that it is not obvious to vulgar eyes, in what manner it is most feelingly inflicted. For this reason it is, that rustic Jobson,* when his wife offends him, takes the strap; and where the strength of arm is with the wife, she generally uses it in a manner to excite her neighbours to lampoon her by a Skimmington.* But I have done my endeavour to set this matter in a clear light, throughout every chapter of my second division.

I once heard a lady declare, that she carefully concealed from her *friends* everything she disliked, as she knew that to be the only chance she had for not being teased and plagued with every little thing that was disagreeable to her. And can anyone, from experience, contradict her prudence, founded, no doubt, on just observation? How have I seen a whole company made uneasy from the screeching of a cork between some person's fingers! the constant drumming upon the table, or shaking of the knee, of another! the hawking* and spawling* of a third! with various inventions of disagreeableness for offending some or all of the senses! To rise a little higher—It is not your violent quarrels, or downright brutal sayings, which sometimes pass in company, that you have reason to fear; it is your sly, malicious reflections, and invidious turns, that may be given to well-meant words, that makes company frequently very disagreeable. The lion and the tiger come not often in our way; or if they did, we should be aware of their teeth and claws; but it is your gnats, your wasps, and, in some countries, your mosquito flies, that are your constant and true tormentors.

I know that many learned and good men have taken great pains to undermine this our noble art, by laying down rules, and giving exemplars, in order to teach mankind to give no offence to anyone, and, instead of being a torment, to be as great a help and comfort to their friends, as it is in their power to be. But with infinite pleasure do I perceive, either that they are not much read, or, at least, that they have not the power of rooting from the human breast that growing sprig of mischief there implanted with our birth; and generally, as we come to years of discretion, flourishing like a green palm tree: yet, to show my great candour and generosity to these my mortal (or rather moral) foes, I will endeavour, as far as my poor recommendation will go, to forward the sale of their books, even among my own pupils. For if, my good scholars, you will guard your minds against the doctrines they intend to teach; if you will consider them as mere amusements; you have my leave to peruse them. Or rather, if you will only remember to observe my orders, in acting in direct opposition to all that a Swift, an Addison, a Richardson, a Fielding,* or any other good ethical writer intended to teach, you may (by referring sometimes to these my rules, as helps to your memory) become as profound adepts in this Art, as any of the readers of Mr Hoyle are in the science of whist.*

Great are the disputes amongst the learned, whether man, as an animal, be a savage and ferocious, or a gentle and social beast. Swift's picture, in his Yahoos,* gives us not a very favourable view of the natural disposition of the animal man; yet I remember not, that he supposes him naturally to delight in tormenting; or does he make him guilty of any vices, but following his brutish appetites. Must not this love of Tormenting therefore be cultivated and cherished? There are many tastes, as that of the olive, the oyster, with several high sauces, cooked up with assafœtida* and the like, which at first are disgustful to the palate, but when once a man has so far depraved his natural taste, as to get a relish for those dainties, there is nothing he is half so fond of.

I can recollect but one kind of brute, that seems to have any notion of this pleasant practice of Tormenting; and that is the cat, when she has got a mouse—She delays the gratification of her hunger, which prompted her to seek for food, and triumphs in her power over her wretched captive—She not only sticks her claws into it, making it feel the sharpness of her teeth (without touching the vitals enough to render it insensible to her tricks), but she tosses it over her head in sport, seems in the highest joy imaginable, and is also, to all appearance, at that very time, the sweetest best-humoured animal in the world. Yet should anything approach her that she fears will rob her of her plaything (holding her prey fast in her teeth), she swears, she growls, and shows all the savage motions of her heart. As soon as her fears are over, she again resumes her sport; and is, in this one instance only, kinder to her victim, than her imitators men, that by death she at last puts a final end to the poor wretch's torments.

Was I to rack my invention and memory for ever, I could not find a more adequate picture of the true lovers of Tormenting than this sportive cat: nor will I tire my reader's patience longer, than to add this farther precept:

Remember always to do unto everyone, what you would least wish to have done unto yourself;* for in this is contained the whole of our excellent *Science*.

FINIS

A FABLE

IN the time when beasts could speak, and write, and read the English language, and were moved with the same passions as men; there was found an old poem, in which was strongly described the misery that is endured, from the entrance of teeth and claws into living flesh. In the strongest colours was painted the pain which the poor sufferer sustains, his agonizing faintness from loss of blood, with the exquisite torment he undergoes, until his heartfelt anguish is relieved by death.

The name of the author was not prefixed to this poem; but on the title-page, at the bottom, was inscribed the letter L.

Its real author not being known, a claim (in the name of their ancestors) was laid to it by all the savage race. The critics take the matter in hand, and endless would have been the debate, had not the letter L, on the title-page, confined the competitors to the lion, the leopard, the lynx, and the lamb.

The lamb, by almost general consent, was instantly thrown out, as knowing nothing of the subjects treated of in the poem. Long were the pleadings of the lion, the leopard, and the lynx, to prove, from the strength of the one, the activity of the other, and the fierceness of the third, that each was best-qualified for writing a pathetic description: till at last the generous horse begged leave to observe—That the poem now contended for, could not be the work of any one of the above claimants, who had roared so loud to prove their title: 'For it is impossible', says he, 'that any beast, that has the feeling which our author shows for the tortured wretches who are torn by savage teeth and claws, should ever make the ravages, which, it is notorious, are daily made by the three fierce competitors before us. The writer of this poem, therefore,' continued he, 'must be no other than the lamb. As it is from suffering, and not from inflicting torments, that the true idea of them is gained.'

EXPLANATORY NOTES

title page: '*Speak Daggers—but use none*'; in Shakespeare's *Hamlet* (III. ii. 387), Hamlet plans a conversation with his mother: 'I will speak daggers to her, but use none.'

Frontispiece: '*Celebrare domestica facta*' (Celebrate domestic affairs): Horace, *Ars Poetica*, l. 287. 'The Cat doth play, | And after slay': perhaps from Benjamin Harris's guide to reading for children, *The New English Tutor* (1705?), 14; or more likely (as Judith Hawley suggests) from T.H.'s *The Child's Guide* (1753), 7. See Judith Hawley (ed.), *The Art of Ingeniously Tormenting* (Bristol: Thoemmes Press, 1994), p. xliv n. 2. In both cases the motto appears as part of a moral alphabet.

3   *Advertisement to the Reader*: the Advertisement was added in the 1757 edition.

5   *Low Countries*: Holland, Belgium, and Luxembourg.

    Inventas aut . . . merendo?: '[or] people who cultivated life through arts they discovered and made others remember them by their desserts'. The passage describes the philosophers who are honoured with a place in the mythical paradise of Elysium.

6   *Dean Swift's instructions*: Jonathan Swift's satire on the conduct of domestic staff, *Directions to Servants* (1745).

    institutes: laws or instructions.

    the jay in the fable: in the fables attributed to the Greek slave Aesop, who lived in the sixth century BC, a jay borrows the fallen feathers from a peacock. But the real peacocks see through his trick and peck away his 'borrowed plumes'.

7   *Nero, Caligula, Phalaris*: the notoriously extravagant and ruthless Roman Emperor Nero (AD 37–68); the cruel, autocratic Roman Emperor Caligula (AD 12–41); and Phalaris, tyrant of Acragas in Sicily from *c*.570 to 554 BC, who infamously roasted his victims alive in a hollow bronze bull.

    bastinado: a beating with a stick or cudgel.

8   *If he be not in parliament, I do*: a Member of Parliament could have pleaded immunity to arrest.

    the Fleet, or King's Bench: the Fleet and the King's Bench Prison were debtors' jails.

9   *this kind of pleasure*: reads 'this kind of happiness' in the 1753 edition.

    a blow on one cheek, will turn the other: see Matthew 5: 39: 'whosoever shall smite thee on thy right cheek, turn to him the other also.'

10 *divines*: clergymen.

   picketing: a military punishment which involved torturing soldiers with a picket, a stake with a pointed top.

   keelhauling: a punishment for seamen which involved lowering the offender under the keel of a ship and hauling him across to the other side.

   the Jew's forfeit of a pound of flesh: in Shakespeare's play, the Jewish moneylender Shylock loans three thousand ducats to Antonio on condition that he forfeit a pound of flesh should he fail to repay them on time.

   a good pretty picking: choice scraps, deceitfully acquired.

11 *well-liken*: i.e. well-liking; thriving and healthy.

13 *heads*: headings.

14 *you must raise your voice, and tell her*: the first edition of 1753 uses indirect speech for the tirade which follows. In 1757, here and elsewhere, inverted commas are added to distinguish the voice of the tormentor from the essayist.

   family: the servants in a household.

   'that you will not hear . . . a good excuse for it': these insults appear in indirect speech in the 1753 edition.

15 *Take great care*: reads 'Be sure' in the 1753 edition.

   rating: berating or chiding.

   But this ingenious method . . . an instance: reads 'To explain myself in this, let me give you an instance' in the 1753 edition.

   chair: a covered chair carried on poles by two men, hired for short-distance travel in towns and cities.

17 *termagant*: an overbearing, quarrelsome woman.

   Ben Jonson's observation: poet and dramatist Ben Jonson (1572?–1637). The pig-woman Ursula in *Bartholomew Fair* (1614) is described by Winwife as 'Mother of the Furies' (ii. v. 77). Alternatively, Collier may be thinking of a line in *The Alchemist* (1610), where Tribulation describes devilish, atheistic alchemists as cooks (iii. i. 21). Cooks are proverbially bad-tempered: see Morris Palmer Tilley, *A Dictionary of the Proverbs in England in the Sixteenth and Seventeenth Centuries* (Ann Arbor: University of Michigan Press, 1950), G222, p. 252 and C634, p. 118.

   slut: a dirty, impudent woman, especially a kitchen-maid.

18 *toad-eater*: a contemptuous term for a dependant or humble friend. As Sarah Fielding explains, 'It is a metaphor taken from a mountebank's boy's eating toads, in order to show his master's skill in expelling poison: It is built on a supposition . . . that people who are so unhappy as to be in a state of dependence, are forced to do the most nauseous things that can be thought on, to please and humour their patrons.' See *The Adventures of David Simple*, bk. 2, ch. 7, ed. Linda Bree (London: Penguin, 2001), 103.

20 *Don't suffer her*: don't allow her.

21 *indulgence to an unfortunate deserving person*: reads 'indulgence to such' in the 1753 edition.

by a friend: reads 'by a person' in the 1753 edition.

22 *Cowley's exclamation . . . his most bitter enemy*: the poet Abraham Cowley (1618–67). In 'Several Discourses by Way of Essays, in Verse and Prose', Cowley reworked Martial's epigram 'Vota tui Breviter'. See *Works* (1668), 86–7, sigs. ²L3ᵛ–L4ʳ (ll. 13–20):

> If there be Man (ye Gods) I ought to Hate
> Dependance and Attendance be his Fate.
> Still let him Busie be, and in a crowd,
> And very much a Slave, and very Proud:
> Thus he perhaps Pow'rful and Rich may grow;
> No matter, O ye Gods! that I'le allow.
> But let him Peace and Freedome never see;
> Let him not love this Life, who loves not Me.

See also Martial, *Epigrams*, bk. I, epigram 55, ed. and trans. D. R. Shackleton Bailey, 3 vols. (Cambridge, Mass. and London: Harvard University Press, 1993), i. 82–3.

23 *numberless families . . . come to decay*: the daughter of a clergyman who fell on hard times, Collier could herself be described as one such dependant.

24 *make love to you*: flirt with you.

looking at her . . . 'I beseech you . . . encouraged to do': this insult appears in indirect speech in the 1753 edition, and the phrase 'looking at her with a mixture of anger and contempt' is omitted.

if she is really an olive beauty: reads 'if 'tis not of the whitest sort' in the 1753 edition.

as white as a cloth: as white as a sheet.

unmeaning: unexpressive.

25 *the words of Butler . . . comes too late*: the poet Samuel Butler (c.1613–80) whose popular two-part satire *Hudibras* was published in 1663–4. The couplets should read as follows:

> And though some critics here cry shame,
> And say our authors are to blame
>
> To which he answered, cruel fate
> Tells me thy counsel comes too late.

See *Hudibras*, ed. John Wilders (Oxford: Clarendon Press, 1967), 40 and 78.

26 *Mistress Minx*: a sly, boldly flirtatious woman.

and, in a soft and gentle accent . . . more than I do: these claims appear in indirect speech in the 1753 edition and the phrase 'in a soft and gentle accent' is omitted.

27 *to walk London streets*: i.e. as a prostitute.

   jargon: baffling mixture.

   sans-pareil: smelling salts carried by ladies; literally 'not having its like' in French.

28 *observations*: reads 'reflections' in the 1753 edition.

29 *chief mark*: main target.

   noddle: nod or shake.

   tricked: artificially adorned or decked.

   prinking: preening, fussing.

   pudden: pudding.

30 *warm exercise*: hard work.

   Dolt, and Mope: blockhead, slow-witted simpleton.

31 *bounce the door*: slam the door.

32 *Billingsgate*: London fish market, famous for the coarse language of its traders.

   St Giles's: the parish of St Giles in the Fields in London was notorious for its poverty and squalor.

   prologue: reads 'speech' in the 1753 edition.

33 *high heads*: eighteenth-century style of arranging powdered hair high above the head with the help of a headdress.

34 *Duris genuit . . . tigres*: 'Caucasus bristling with rough rocks brought you into being and Hyrcanian tigers tendered their udders.' In this passage Dido first reproaches and then threatens Aeneas for planning to leave Carthage.

35 *ancient Rome . . . life and death*: the practice of infanticide, or the abandonment of unwanted newborns, was common in ancient Rome.

   Purchased slaves are not allowed: in fact slavery was not declared illegal in England until 1772. See Audrey Bilger (ed.), *An Essay on the Art of Ingeniously Tormenting* (Peterborough, Ont.: Broadview Press, 2003), 70 n. 1.

37 *low enough*: i.e. in terms of class or social status.

   highest: richest.

38 *small-beer*: weak, inferior beer.

   hashes: a dish consisting of pieces of meat cooked earlier, warmed up with gravy.

39 *Bk. I, ch. 9*: Francis Coventry's satire on the flaws of middle-class English society, *The History of Pompey the Little: Or, The Life and Adventures of a*

Lap-Dog (1751). In the chapter Collier mentions, four young children maliciously drown kittens and behead magpies (pp. 82–3).

inculcate early . . . the love of cruelty: reads 'inculcate the love of cruelty' in the 1753 edition.

wake: festival.

grown up to men or women's estate: i.e. to adulthood.

40 *for how must an old Harlowe . . . kind words!*: in Samuel Richardson's novel *Clarissa* (1747–8), Clarissa's father and other members of her family promise her jewels and gifts if she agrees to marry their chosen suitor, Mr Solmes. See *Clarissa, or the History of a Young Lady*, ed. Angus Ross (Harmondsworth: Penguin, 1985), letter 13, p. 80.

the behaviour of old Western . . . a deserving child: in Henry Fielding's novel *The History of Tom Jones, A Foundling* (1749), Squire Western exerts pressure on his daughter Sophia to marry the undeserving Mr Blifil. See *Tom Jones*, ed. John Bender and Simon Stern (Oxford World's Classics, 1996), esp. bk VI, ch. 4, pp. 245–7.

41 *the Tormenting children*: i.e. the tormenting of children.

42 *if Solomon . . . Train up your child, &c.*: see Proverbs 22: 6: 'Train up a child in the way he should go: and when he is old, he will not depart from it.' King Solomon is renowned for his wisdom in the Old Testament.

43 *who are not governed*: reads 'are governed' in the 1753 edition. The correction made in the 1757 edition makes better sense.

44 *spleen*: ill temper.

45 *indifference, will do very well*: reads 'indifference, if not dislike, to your own home, will do very well' in the 1753 edition.

It has been observed . . . to the good: in a similar proverb, 'We men of intrigues observe stricter faith to one another than honest folk'. See Burton Stephenson, *The Home Book of Proverbs, Maxims and Familiar Phrases* (New York: Macmillan, 1948); Bilger (ed.), *The Art of Ingeniously Tormenting*, 79 n. 1.

justly: reads 'fairly' in the 1753 edition.

As things are now circumstanced: reads 'Yet still, as things are now circumstanced' in the 1753 edition.

46 *arise . . . the tender affection of his wife*: reads 'arise, not from his exterior authority, but from the affection of his wife' in the 1753 edition.

48 *coquette-behaviour*: flirtatious behaviour.

most of our comedies since the Restoration: Charles II was restored to the throne of England in 1660. The comedies which flourished around this time were notorious for their licentious wit and urbanity.

49 *Aut videt, aut vidisse putat*: 'he either sees or believes he has seen'. From the episode in Book VI where Aeneas encounters Dido's spirit in the underworld.

49 *equipage*: domestic accoutrements, especially crockery.

    a work before half-finished: reads 'a work, perhaps, before, half-finished' in the 1753 edition.

50 *frowardness*: contrariness.

    a cause of cruelty against him, in Doctors Commons: the courts attached to the society of ecclesiastical lawyers known as Doctors' Commons, located near St Paul's Cathedral in London. These courts handled civil cases, including domestic disputes, and Collier's brother Arthur practised law there.

    Ecclesiasticus 25: 22: this note was added in the 1757 edition. 'A woman, if she maintain her husband, is full of anger, impudency, and much reproach.' Like many of her contemporaries, Collier mistakenly attributes the Book of Ecclesiasticus to Solomon.

51 *rubs*: obstacles.

52 *old saw*: saying.

    the Spectator, 'You are all . . . to you?': *The Spectator* was a periodical published between 1711 and 1714 by Richard Steele and Joseph Addison. Collier's quotation comes from an article by Steele in no. 212 (2 November 1711) in which a man complains about his jealous wife: 'if I offered to go abroad, she would get between me and the door, kiss me, and say she could not part with me; then down again I sat. In a day or two, after this first pleasant step towards confining me, she declared to me, that I was all the world to her, and she thought she ought to be all the world to me.' See Donald F. Bond (ed.), *The Spectator*, 5 vols. (Oxford: Clarendon Press, 1965; reissued 1987), ii. 329.

53 *own yourself*: confess yourself.

    curtain-lecture: a reproach given from a wife to a husband while they are in bed.

    nice: difficult.

55 *before your union with him*: reads 'before you was married' in the 1753 edition.

    insult: reads 'nose', i.e. confront, in the 1753 edition.

56 *Vauxhall, Ranelagh*: pleasure gardens in London where balls and concerts were held and people met to socialize. Vauxhall Gardens in Lambeth were the most famous, and Ranelagh Gardens lay on the east side of Chelsea Hospital.

58 *post-chaise*: a travelling carriage for two or four persons, drawn by horses.

60 *An ingenious French writer . . . many more*: 'De l'amitié', an essay by Michel de Montaigne (1553–92) first published in *Essais* (1580) and translated as 'Of Friendship' or 'Of Affectionate Relationships'. Montaigne divides the affections people feel for one another into various categories, such as the love between brothers, acquaintances, fathers and sons, or

husbands and wives. See *The Complete Essays*, trans. M. A. Screech (London: Penguin, 1991; repr. 2003), 205–19.

Pylades . . . Pollux: according to Greek legend, Pylades and Orestes were inseparable friends; in some versions of the story, Pylades marries Orestes' sister Electra. The twin heroes Castor and Pollux, famously devoted to one another, were immortalized by Zeus in the constellation of Gemini.

as was shown from Jonathan to David: Jonathan was the eldest son of King Saul and the loving companion of David. See 1 Samuel 20.

gudgeons: small fish often used for bait; and, by extension, credulous or gullible people.

physiognomy: the art of judging a person's character by reading the face.

61 *Life of Jonathan Wild*: in Henry Fielding's novel *The Life of Jonathan Wild the Great* (1743), the innocent Thomas Heartfree is persecuted by his villainous former school friend, the thief and highwayman Jonathan Wild.

62 *those who are in want*: reads 'those who want' in the 1753 edition.

See Mr Orgueil . . . ch. 4: The *Adventures of David Simple, Volume the Last* (1753) was the sequel to *The Adventures of David Simple* (1744), the first novel by Collier's friend and collaborator Sarah Fielding. In the chapter cited, David Simple asks for assistance from his so-called friend Mr Orgueil, but is offered only useless advice. See *The Adventures of David Simple*, ed. Bree, 330–1.

63 *harrow*: a heavy frame set with iron teeth used to prepare ploughed land before sowing.

Familiar Letters, vol. i, letter 5, vol. ii, letter 21: the publication of Sarah Fielding's *The Adventures of David Simple* was followed by *Familiar Letters Between the Principal Characters in David Simple* (1747). In the first letter Collier cites, Cynthia writes to Camilla about a man who receives an annual income of £600 upon the death of his father who has left no provision for his other son and daughter. The sole inheritor provides his siblings with a pitiful allowance, sufficient only to keep them from starvation (vol. i, pp. 139–40). In the second letter, from Cratander to Lysimachus, Rufus declines to help his stepmother and two stepsisters after his father has died. Upon the death of his stepmother, however, he offers her daughters just enough money to prevent them from receiving help from any other source (vol. ii, pp. 18–20).

64 *friendship with each other*: reads 'friendship' in the 1753 edition.

67 *'you can get nothing done for you, unless you do it yourself'*: this phrase appears as direct speech in 1757, and indirect speech in 1753.

proffered service, &c.: 'Proffered service stinks', i.e. services or wares freely offered are not worth having. See Tilley, *A Dictionary of the Proverbs in England*, S252, p. 594. Collier omits the final verb in the interests of decency.

68 *There is a story . . . the tip of his ear*: Sarah Fielding, *The Adventures of David Simple*, bk. 4, ch. 4, ed. Bree, p. 242.

   this worthy man: reads 'this man' in the 1753 edition.

69 *ribband*: ribbon.

70 *to own the truth*: to own up to the truth.

72 *backstroke*: a counterblow.

73 *worked your friends to oil*: i.e. lubricated them, made them pliable.

   Fool'd them to the top of their bent: in *Hamlet*, iii. ii. 375, Hamlet complains of Polonius, Rosencrantz, and Guildenstern, 'They fool me to the top of my bent'. Sarah Fielding quotes the same line in *The Adventures of David Simple*, bk. 2, ch. 7, ed. Bree, p. 103.

74 *Should the person . . . anything with you*: reads 'Should your friend seldom dispute anything with you' in the 1753 edn.

   the patience of Job: in the Book of Job, Job is tested by Satan with a series of disasters, but retains an unwavering faith in God.

   Talem progenies . . . Pollux: 'If that old race of men had produced such a character, Theseus would have abandoned Pirithous, Pylades would have deserted Orestes in umbrage, Pollux would have hated Castor.' In *Against Rufinus*, the Latin poet Claudian Claudianus (AD 395–404) attacks the magistrate and rehearses his murder. Each of the three pairs of men in the quotation was famous for their close friendship. (Collier mistakenly references l. 107; this has been corrected.)

75 *Says Dean Swift . . . take a bit*: Jonathan Swift's poem *Cadenus and Vanessa*, first published in 1726, ll. 776–9. See *Major Works*, ed. David Woolley (Oxford: Oxford University Press, 1984; rev. 2003), 352–3.

76 *great uneasiness*: reads 'great pain and uneasiness' in the 1753 edition.

77 *notwithstanding the amiable character . . . a love to our sport*: reads 'I think, in her, I spy some marks of a love to our sport' in the 1753 edition.

78 *the flying squadron*: 'A division of a fleet forming one body under the command of a flag-officer' (*OED*).

   folio: the largest size of printed book, made up of sheets of paper folded once.

80 *a living example of a person*: Augusta of Saxe-Coburg, Princess of Wales (1719–72). Collier wrote that 'the book is in an oblique manner addressed to the Princess of Wales by the compliment intended for her in the 4th chapter of the Second Part'. See *The Correspondence of Henry and Sarah Fielding*, ed. Martin C. Battestin and Clive T. Probyn (Oxford: Clarendon Press, 1993), p. xxxiii n. 38. I owe this reference to Bilger (ed.), *The Art of Ingeniously Tormenting*, 112 n. 1.

83 *punctilio*: punctiliousness, petty formalities of behaviour.

84 *wink at*: turn a blind eye to.

capuchins: cloaks with hoods, worn by women.

tippets: short capes or scarves for the neck and shoulders.

86 *Sadler's Wells*: a theatre in London's Islington, famous for the debauchery of its clientele.

manteau-makers: dressmakers.

railly: ridicule.

87 *a brother of the Masonry*: members of the fraternity of the Masons, or Freemasons, identified one another by a secret set of signs.

arcana: mysteries.

tower of Babel: in Genesis 11: 1–9, the human race attempts to construct a tower as high as the heavens.

88 *if she happens to like walking leisurely*: reads 'if she likes walking leisurely' in the 1753 edition.

glasses: windows.

tilt: awning made of canvas.

89 *you are their queen*: reads 'you as their queen' in the 1753 edition.

coach and chaise: a chaise was a small travelling carriage; a coach rather bigger.

Windsor . . . Esher: Windsor is a town by the River Thames to the west of London, and the location of Windsor Castle; Esher is an area in Surrey, south-west of London.

the Duke of Newcastle's, and Mr Pelham's: Thomas Pelham-Holles (1693–1768), Duke of Newcastle upon Tyne, prime minister of Great Britain from 1754 to 1756 and minister of finances from 1757 to 1762. Henry Pelham (1694–1754), brother of the Duke of Newcastle and prime minister from 1743 to 1754. Their 'seats', or residences, were notable examples of fine houses in the district.

Hampton Court: in Surrey, home of the Tudor palace and gardens of Hampton Court.

90 *knotting-bag*: a bag holding materials for lacework or macramé, the craft of knitting knots together.

91 *prospects*: views of the landscape.

92 '*that no fine prospect . . . from walking*': this phrase appears as indirect speech in the 1753 edition.

a sweat: a state of anxiety.

Claremont: Claremont Park, a landscape garden.

'*that you will not . . . left by yourself*': this phrase appears as indirect speech in the 1753 edition.

ombre: a fashionable game of cards.

93 '*that you are so low-spirited . . . part of the company*': this phrase appears as indirect speech in the 1753 edition.

'*that you hoped . . . your husband's sisters*': this phrase appears as indirect speech in the 1753 edition.

as you possibly can . . . the least pleased: reads 'as possible, without seeming in the least pleased' in the 1753 edition.

'*that you suppose . . . the young fellows*': this phrase appears as indirect speech in the 1753 edition.

after your husband . . . Mr Pelham's elegant gardens: reads 'your husband, and the rest of the company, will give up all thoughts of seeing Mr Pelham's elegant gardens' in the 1753 edition.

the beauties there, painted by Sir Godfrey Kneller: Sir Godfrey Kneller (1646–1723) was a painter celebrated for his portraits of noblemen and court 'beauties'.

94 *that is, you may put off all their proposals*: reads 'that is, putting it off' in the 1753 edition.

Now is your time to take all opportunities: reads 'Take all opportunities' in the 1753 edition.

Richmond: a town on the Thames, south of the city of London.

Kingston: a town on the south bank of the Thames.

you may declare . . . never felt before: reads 'you may be suddenly taken with such a panic upon the water, that, you may say, you never felt before' in the 1753 edition.

Twickenham: another town on the Thames, south of London.

drops: medicine, administered in small quantities.

95 *Montagu House*: Montagu House in London's Bloomsbury district was designed by the English architect Robert Hooke and built in 1675–9 for Ralph Montagu (1638–1709), 1st Duke of Montagu. It was rebuilt after a fire in 1686, and demolished in the 1840s.

tilting: fighting or duelling.

and like Chevy Chase . . . the Pleasure of that day: English ballad entitled *The Hunting of the Cheviot*, commemorating the battle of Otterburn in 1388. See *The English and Scottish Popular Ballads*, 5 vols., ed. Francis James Child (vol. iii, ballad 162). Cited in Bilger (ed.), *The Art of Ingeniously Tormenting*, 125 n. 2.

97 *That great emperor Marcus Antoninus . . . left to the world*: Marcus Aurelius Antoninus (AD 121–80), Roman emperor from AD 161 to 180. His *Thoughts* or *Meditations* comprise twelve books of ethical aphorisms. See *The Meditations of Marcus Aurelius Antoninus*, trans. John Jackson (Oxford: Clarendon Press, 1906).

rustic Jobson: a country bumpkin.

Skimmington: a noisy procession accompanied by the banging of pots and pans, held in towns or villages to humiliate unfaithful husbands or wives. Effigies were often paraded through the streets; Thomas Hardy describes a Skimmington ride in *The Mayor of Casterbridge* (1886).

hawking: noisy clearing of the throat.

spawling: spitting.

98 *a Fielding*: either Sarah or Henry Fielding, both of whom wrote 'ethical' fictions.

Mr Hoyle are in the science of whist: Edmond Hoyle (1671/2–1769) wrote *A Short Treatise on the Game of Whist* (1742), a book of rules and tactics for the popular card game. Henry Fielding mentions Hoyle's book in *Tom Jones*, bk. 13, ch. 5, ed. Bender and Stern, p. 616.

Swift's picture, in his Yahoos: in part 4 of *Gulliver's Travels* (1726) by Jonathan Swift (1667–1745), Gulliver travels to the country of the Houyhnhnms where he is horrified to encounter the Yahoos, or human savages, in a land populated by horses endowed with dignity and reason.

assafœtida: or asafoetida, a strong-tasting gum used in medicine and cooking.

99 *Remember always to do unto everyone . . . unto yourself*: Collier reverses the familiar precept from Matthew 7: 12, 'all things whatsoever ye would that men should do to you, do ye even so to them'.

Women's Writing 1778–1838

JAMES BOSWELL   **Life of Johnson**

FRANCES BURNEY   **Cecilia**
Evelina

JOHN CLELAND   **Memoirs of a Woman of Pleasure**

DANIEL DEFOE   **A Journal of the Plague Year**
Moll Flanders
Robinson Crusoe

HENRY FIELDING   **Joseph Andrews and Shamela**
Tom Jones

WILLIAM GODWIN   **Caleb Williams**

OLIVER GOLDSMITH   **The Vicar of Wakefield**

ELIZABETH INCHBALD   **A Simple Story**

SAMUEL JOHNSON   **The History of Rasselas**

ANN RADCLIFFE   **The Italian**
The Mysteries of Udolpho

SAMUEL RICHARDSON   **Pamela**

TOBIAS SMOLLETT   **The Adventures of Roderick Random**
The Expedition of Humphry Clinker

LAURENCE STERNE   **The Life and Opinions of Tristram**
Shandy, Gentleman
A Sentimental Journey

JONATHAN SWIFT   **Gulliver's Travels**
A Tale of a Tub and Other Works

HORACE WALPOLE   **The Castle of Otranto**

MARY WOLLSTONECRAFT   **Mary and The Wrongs of Woman**
A Vindication of the Rights of Woman

The Oxford World's Classics Website

www.worldsclassics.co.uk

- Information about new titles
- Explore the full range of Oxford World's Classics
- Links to other literary sites and the main OUP webpage
- Imaginative competitions, with bookish prizes
- Peruse the Oxford World's Classics Magazine
- Articles by editors
- Extracts from Introductions
- A forum for discussion and feedback on the series
- Special information for teachers and lecturers

www.worldsclassics.co.uk

American Literature

British and Irish Literature

Children's Literature

Classics and Ancient Literature

Colonial Literature

Eastern Literature

European Literature

History

Medieval Literature

Oxford English Drama

Poetry

Philosophy

Politics

Religion

The Oxford Shakespeare